Pilots Progress

the highs and lows of a single engine flyer

Martin Leusby

About the Author

Martin Leusby is a private pilot with over 3000 hours flying experience, based in South-East England.

He has competed in sporting aviation and represented his country, and now flies on behalf of the emergency services – which is quite unusual on a private licence.

Martin has written articles for aviation magazines including such as Pilot Magazine, Flyer, and AOPA. During the recent pandemic lockdown, he wrote his first novella – an aviation crime thriller targeted at fellow pilots "The Airborne Ghost". Following good reviews from the aviation press, he penned his memoir of a lifetime interest in aviation and almost forty years of private flying.

Fellow pilots, would-be pilots, and aviation enthusiasts will all appreciate his relaxed style and sense of humour – and learn just how much can be achieved with commitment, and how much enjoyment can be had from flying!

About this Book

"And (almost) all in one aeroplane! The author has enjoyed a special degree of adventure in General Aviation"- **Phillip Whiteman, Editor, Pilot Magazine**

"Spurred on by the positive reception to his first aviation thriller, "The Airborne Ghost", Martin has set about recording the trials and tribulations of progressing his PPL skills. The result is "Pilots Progress", a fun book, with a quirky array of tales - **Ed Hicks, Editor, Flyer Magazine**

Introduction

I am tempted to say that I learnt to fly at the best possible time, but any time is the right time. To gain a licence is always a stretch in more ways than one and continuing to make use of it, and to progress, is sometimes not easy. But whenever the opportunity to become an aviator arises – you should grasp it with both hands.

You will be a rare person if you regret doing it, and you may always regret it if you do not.

There will be challenges along the way, possibly not least with the authorities, but also the most enormous amount of fun. My enjoyment has not stopped yet and has no signs of doing so.

I trust you will enjoy what follows – I did.

Martin Leusby, Private Pilot.

P.S. For any non-pilots reading this (or pilots unfamiliar with old-fashioned terms), there is a glossary at the back of the book where you can look up acronyms and expressions you may not know.

I blame my Mother….

Being born in the fifties (1950 to be precise), I was the usual kid who enjoyed watching steam trains whilst they were still around and making the occasional Airfix model plane (Frog kits were also acceptable). I liked going to primary school, but never had any idea what it would lead to, and no thoughts of any career, until Mother made her mistake.

We were attending the Barton Air Show, which featured much of the Lancashire Aero Club and included the opportunity to take a joyride in a Piper Tri-Pacer (or was it a Piper Colt?) for the princely sum of £5. It was to be the most expensive £5 my mother ever spent on me - for her in the short term, and for me for the rest of my life.

After a short time in the air, probably just one circuit, my mind was made up and I was going to be a Pilot! There was no thought about what would be necessary to achieve this, such as education, money etc., it was just what was going to happen. There were some even more basic obstacles, mainly that I was far too young and not even at secondary school yet, but nothing could deter me from the ambition.

My mother (and father, of course) immediately felt the impact. If I could not fly yet, the least I could do was watch others doing it, and with Ringway Airport (now Manchester International) only 12 miles away by bike, I disappeared every evening and most of the weekend. At the weekends I would go even further, another 12 miles or so, to watch the Vulcans at the Avro factory at Woodford.

My prolonged absence did not bode well for my homework requirements, and the parents decided they would have to cut a deal with me. I would have to ensure I did enough work to get good grades, or privileges (the bike) would be withdrawn. I complied. However, even at that young age, I became a negotiator, and when they wanted to go on driving holidays and with my being too young to be left at home, they had to agree on routes that would keep me amused. This was great, as it meant that any trips in the Morris 1000 usually ended up as a tour of airfields, wherever in the country we went. Superb examples included a trip to Yorkshire timed to coincide with the SSAFA Air Show at RAF Finningley (now Doncaster Sheffield Airport). An eight Vulcan scramble was most impressive, and made the earth move! A tour of Scotland found us at Inverness when they were filming 633 Squadron with Mosquitos and a Mitchell B-25 as camera ship. I still have a picture of my dad stood in front of a Mossie riddled with bullet-holes (painted on, of course).

Countrywide, I had lots of opportunities to be underlining registrations of aircraft I had seen in my Ian Allen Civil Aircraft Registrations book, and a similar amateur-produced list of RAF aircraft, and Ringway still beckoned but not quite as often. With homework done, I would often cycle up there to see night arrivals. Somehow news would get around if something special was happening – such as the first Trident (G-ARPB) to arrive. It was also at night that I fell in love with my all-time favourite airliner, the Super Constellation, when the Portuguese airline TAP paid a visit. Mr Lockheed had created the most elegant lines of an aircraft imaginable, and I still lust after flying in one.

In those days, security was not a problem at airports, and they encouraged spectators with whole rooftop terraces available for viewing. At Ringway it could be expensive as one turnstile let one into the Domestic piers, and there was a further one to reach the International pier – and each one was a shilling (5p to any younger readers) to pass through. Fortunately, the population was a lot slimmer in those days, and two of the middle bars of the turnstile were wider apart than the others, so if agile enough and with no-one watching, you could pull yourself up and swing your legs through the wider-spaced bars, then slide through into the other side for free. Naturally, I will deny ever doing this.

Pleasurable as all this free admission and aircraft-watching was, it was not getting me closer to my career goal, so in between I knuckled down and really worked. My parents had pointed out that I would need good qualifications, so I was pleased that when I took an entrance exam for Manchester Grammar, I was awarded a scholarship. Good job, because the bank of mum and dad could never have afforded the fees for a direct grant school – just the uniform was a stretch.

Having to travel to Fallowfield each day by bus took time, as did the associated homework, so I needed to find something closer to home to get my aviation "fix". The answer was 318 Squadron (Sale and Altrincham) Air Training Corps, which I joined in 1964.

Reporting as a Cadet

My RAF Form 3822 (Record of Service) shows a subsequent 200 hours+ attendance each year at the weekly "parades", where we were coached by a mixture of RAF(VR) officers and Civilian Instructors. Syllabuses included theory of flight, engines and airframes, and the dreaded drill square. With decent application, the plan was to qualify as 1st Class Cadet, followed by Leading Cadet, then Senior Cadet.

But whilst learning about things aeronautical was interesting, the real bonus was the visits and trips out we were allowed on. As a lowly 1st Class Cadet, July 1964 found me issued with a free rail warrant and on a train to RAF Honington for a week-long camp. We were billeted in dormitories, well-fed and our contribution to the costs was just a shilling per day. For this we visited all sorts of airfield operations including the flight-line of Handley Page Victors – both V-bombers and tanker conversions. Two days after arrival, I had my first flight in Chipmunk WP837, and three days later another flight in a venerable Avro Anson, TX185. This was a once only event as four years later the Anson was withdrawn from RAF service. In the same week, I fired my first 10 rounds from a .303 rifle, and by the time I got home, the bruising on my shoulder was just starting to subside!

Another highlight of the week was a visit to nearby RAF Lakenheath. Occupied by USAF 48 Fighter Wing, it was a "Little America" with every convenience, even bowling alleys, to make personnel feel at home. Currency was US Dollars, so as we had none, anything provided to us (food and lane hire) was free.

Even more exciting were their F-100D Super Sabres, which were thrilling to watch. Overall, it was not a bad week for the equivalent of today's 35p.

I managed another half-hour of Chipmunk flight (WP973) a couple of months later at Woodvale. We went by coach, as a squadron, and sat around gossiping whilst waiting our turn to fly. Before my turn, I watched a superb aerobatic display overhead by one of the Chippies. Shortly after, our Sergeant, Norman Sheriff, returned from his Air Experience flight and we all told him that he had missed a brilliant exhibition. "No, I didn't" he said, and promptly emptied what was left of his stomach contents onto the tarmac in front of us. When I was subsequently asked if I wanted to do aerobatics, I agreed "but nothing too extreme".

By February 1965 I was a Leading Cadet and flew in another Woodvale Chipmunk WP786. I missed summer camp that year (which would have been RAF St. Mawgan) due to a mild attack of rheumatic fever, from which I recovered quickly, but which would become a showstopper at some time in the future.

That summer, my parents who were wanting a holiday that was not aviation-related, deemed me old enough to travel without them. John Town, my aircraft-spotting buddy from Stretford and I had been loaned a copy of a diary kept by older spotters we met, that was effectively a guidebook to airfields around the country that they had cycled to, and even showed where they stayed. Our bikes were put to good use. We loaded them onto a train so we could start a lot further south, and then worked our way through the counties to home. It was remarkable how many airfields existed and how close they were to each other, and we averaged five airfields a day.

What is more, the "guide" included hidden gems such as a Pou-de-Ciel in the rafters of a barn, and other wrecks and relics if you knew where to look. At nights we would stay at the local Youth Hostel and that first year we covered 700 miles in 10 days. Our bikes were nothing special, just regular sit up and beg style, but we were young, fit and keen.

The following year we would see many of the fields we had missed, and that year did 900 miles in 7 days. Then John moved away, and I needed a new companion. John Nicholson was a corporal in my ATC unit, and him not being a cyclist, we decided to hitch-hike our way around. We did it in ATC uniform which seemed to help us get lifts fairly easily, and before dusk we would ask farmers if we could sleep in their barn. Nearly all we asked said yes, provided we had no matches or cigarettes, which we did not. A few rearranged bales of straw and we had individual nests and there was always water nearby – often our washbasins were upturned milk churn lids, and many a farmer's wife cooked us a breakfast for little or no charge.

On this trip we had written ahead to lots of airfields (many RAF) and told them of our tour, and could we come and visit? Almost unfailingly they agreed, but one notable exception was Cambridge who told us not to come. Despite that we were passing so it seemed sensible to see what we could find in the largest hangar. Nowadays I would never trespass, but we were callow youths at the time.

We had been looking at the Canberras for some time before we were spotted and questioned as to what we were doing. "Does Mr Marshall know you are here?" "We did write and ask" was all we could honestly say – then we were ejected and told to never come back.

This was quite different to the RAF stations. They had welcomed us with open arms, and even showed us around their private museums such as that at Colerne. It was there that we were allowed to sit in the cockpit of the first RAF Hercules that had arrived just two days earlier from USA. Many of them fed us too.

Another sweet memory was the barn overlooking the end of the runway at Hurn. We were woken to the sound of Sea Hawks being started. We watched as they unfolded their wings, taxied towards us to the runway end and then took to the skies. These were the last operational Sea Hawks and were flown by Airwork Ltd for the Navy's "black" Fleet Requirement Unit. They were retired in 1969.

Climbing the Ranks

By November 1965, I was a Senior Cadet and flew another Woodvale Chippie, WP789. So only two flights that year, but the following February, we were at RAF Sealand to try the delights of gliding. Sedbergh WB927 and Cadet XN194 gave me a circuit each. Another visit to Sealand in June brought me my RAF Marksman Badge on the .303 rifle. This time I pushed the butt hard into my shoulder (and with a beret for cushioning) and managed the prescribed grouping of 5 rounds under an old halfpenny.

By then I had been made up to Corporal (the peak of my ATC career), and the reward in July was a week's camp at RAF Wildenrath, Germany. To get there, I was given a rail warrant to reach Gatwick where I met the other lucky cadets from all over UK, and we all flew direct to Wildenrath on a chartered British United BAC 1-11 G-ASJE – my first jet! Return was to be a little less exciting on Viscount G-APTC, but it was still flying. Obviously, an overseas trip was way more expensive than a UK camp, but somehow, I managed to stump up the grand sum of £8 (covering rail, flights, accommodation etc).

Whilst there we visited the two Canberra squadrons – one nuclear-armed and the other photoreconnaissance. Part of the entertainment was a road trip to the site of the Dambusters attack at Mohne – some 2 hours away. Back at base, and bereft of any Chipmunks, we were treated to a flight in Army Air Corps Beaver XP808. The pilot had just returned from Malaya (his description, as it had recently become Malaysia). Operating there from tiny, rough strips, he decided he would show us the STOL capabilities of the Beaver, landing between the potholes of a disused runway nearby. I was lucky enough to get the right-hand seat, and the attitudes experienced were distinctly thrilling.

Only ten days after return from Germany, I managed to find another seven shillings (35p) to attend the camp at RAF Thorney Island, and get another unusual aircraft in my Form 3822 – Argosy XN858. Again, we had outings and one was to the RAF Tangmere flight-line, where they were still flying the ungainly Beverleys. (Thorney Island was eventually closed by the RAF, but the runways remain and very occasionally they have a fly-in. Who knew that 48 years later I would land my own aircraft there?).

Overall, it had been a great year, but with O-levels out of the way, it was time to get my head down and get the necessary A-levels, so I handed back my uniform and equipment in December 1966.

RAF Assessment at Biggin Hill

If I was going to do all that work, I needed to know that they wanted me, preferably as a pilot of a Lightning! I applied to the RAF and made the trip from Cheshire to Biggin for a two (or was it three?) day assessment. Armed with my signed-off Form 3822, and O-level results, I took the aptitude tests, medical, eyesight and colour-blindness tests and passed with flying colours.

Before I left Biggin, the deal was made that I would receive a Special Flying Award whilst continuing my studies. This meant they would pay for me to gain my Private Pilot Licence whilst at school. I would then go on to university for my degree, and a place at Cranwell would await my results. Elated, I took the train home.

It was only three weeks later that the bomb dropped. Following "further investigation of your medical history" they determined that although I was unharmed by the short episode of rheumatic fever, there was a slight chance I could get it again (and a serious attack could cause heart murmurs), so were not prepared to waste money training me, and declared me unfit for all forms of RAF service. I could not even be an ordinary airman, doing anything on her Majesty's Service, and of course, the Special Flying Award was withdrawn.

Anyone who has ever had a boyhood ambition foiled can imagine the hurt this caused. Schoolwork went to pot. I discovered the Rink Café near the Grammar School, their pinball machine, cigarettes, and eventually girls. So busy was I that it was difficult to find time to attend classes. The damage was really done when my parents attended a parent evening and asked how I was doing, and my form teacher replied with "I was going to ask you – we haven't seen him for 3 months". Manchester Grammar really only wanted Oxbridge candidates, so it was agreed that I should find another route to education, and I switched my school for Salford College of Technology.

I made the mistake of changing subjects slightly, expanding from Physic-with-Chemistry to separate Basic Physics, Basic Chemistry, Basic Maths and Elective Chemistry. It did not work, and I only got O-level passes in the A-level exams. I had had a summer job at my father's works – working as a lab assistant, whilst awaiting results, and with no prospect of university, it was decided that temporary would become permanent and I could try to get HNC Chemistry on day release. This made sense as I could relate the education to my job, although it was not the job of choice.

I need to earn enough to fly!

The transition from £6.25 per week to permanent pay of £9.15 was not going to make a big enough difference. It gradually increased over time, but so did my commitments. Not least was a fiancée, Jean, with whom I committed to buy our first house. Laboratory Assistant was not the role to fund it, so I took a part-time job selling equity-linked life assurance and became rather good at it. The commission was more than I earned in the day job!

By day I was developing industrial adhesives (primarily for wallcoverings) and by night, making money. Then our Chemical Products Division decided they needed a new sales representative in the South of England. They wanted someone who was also technical, and when they looked at options, found that I had sold all of them equity-linked life assurance and would therefore fit the bill.

About to be married in six weeks, I had to put the house we had bought in Radcliffe on the market and find somewhere suitable and almost identical – which we found near Bedford - at just twice the price (but it did have a garage). We had grovelled to get a £5,000 mortgage, but with the firm backing me, £10,000 was miraculously available (as was a bridging loan that they covered). Meanwhile I had to work the area, staying in London for six weeks, then marry and move immediately. The massive salary increase was a whole £20 per year – but I got a company car, which made all the difference.

Again, commission was most important. I worked so hard for a year that after 12 months, every wallcovering distributor in my area was selling my product, and I could do no more. One of my customers needed a wallcovering salesman, and I was poached!

It was a long slog to learn this new business, and I was never able to afford flying lessons, but after being poached again, things got better. By then we had moved to a bigger house near Huntingdon, and we were happy to be in an active aviation environment, constantly overflown by Canberras from RAF Wyton, and everything from F-100D Super Sabres, F5 Tigers and eventually A10 Warthogs from the USAF at RAF Alconbury. Even a U2 on occasions. At evenings and weekends, I was surrounded by aviation, and during my daily travels for work, lunch would often be taken at an aerodrome near wherever I was visiting (or any nearby museums – as long as they contained aeroplanes).

Eventually my wife despaired of my looking skywards all the time and made the right call "Just go and get lessons!". What a woman!

Peterborough Conington

Spookily, her boss Eddie Comber also wanted to learn. Eddie and I weighed up the options and decided that the nearest was Conington, and we should have a go. June 1984 was a long time after my ATC flights, but I finally got to control an aeroplane again. In this case it was Cessna 152 Aerobat G-BFKF, which I stayed with through my learning, but with just a couple of lessons in another 152 G-BGNT. It took me two months and about 13 flying hours to go solo. As I took off that very first time on my own, it was disconcerting for the instructor's door to open of its own accord, and a noisy circuit ensued.

Throughout my lessons the learning curve wavered as it must for everyone, but it was all exciting, and I made some real friendships with fellow students, one of whom was Alan Walton (more later).

By October 1984 I had amassed some 20 hours and still had not left the circuit but had practised force landings. Then disaster struck.

Not in the air but driving to work on a Monday morning when my Ford Orion hit a lorry head-on. I cannot remember the accident, nor the following 10 days when I was in intensive care. The photographs in the local paper that I saw later, showed a Ford about two-thirds of its original length, and minus the roof which had been removed to cut me out.

The net effect of the impact was two broken ankles, a broken knee, two broken femurs, a broken wrist and shoulder, and my ribs went through my liver. Apparently when you break so much you can have a fat embolism which can quickly kill you – hence why I was completely out of it for ten days. Having got past that, I underwent a series of lengthy operations to bolt me back together, with the biggest being a number of plates (and 24 screws) bracketing the shattered femur bones. The same team that repaired motorcyclist Barry Sheane after a horrendous crash, worked on me.

Friends and family rallied round, and I was never short of visitors, and these included Eddie Comber who in an effort to cheer me up, declared that as soon as I was fit enough, the two of us were to start building our own aircraft, a Rand KR-2, so that when we qualified, we would have something to fly. It seemed like a good idea, so I agreed.

Amazingly, I was able to leave hospital after about three months, albeit in a wheelchair. Lots of return trips for physiotherapy, and eventually I learned to walk again.

When I had been "poached" for the latest job, I had come to a rather unusual arrangement. Having made rather a lot of money for previous employers, but still not earning enough, I had wanted to see some of the profits myself, so had entered a partnership with a Limited Company. I was paid for technical assistance by that company but remained self-employed so I could benefit from my own sales, which the company facilitated by use of their warehouse and systems for an agreed fee. This meant I needed to be back at work as soon as I could stand. This was to be important for my future flying.

Life became work during the week, and home-building from plans in Eddie's garage at weekends. Spookily my initials were about to come up in sequence in new aircraft registrations, and after a friendly conversation the CAA allocated G-BMFL to our just-started build, without any fee.

It took eight months for me to be fit enough to continue flying lessons, and I had to fly dual for three hours before they allowed me to repeat Exercise 14 – so I have two first solos recorded in my logbook.

I had finally amassed 50 hours when I took the test at the end of October 1985, then waited for issue of my poo-brown CAA PPL. Whilst it was on its way, I had a call from hospital wanting me to go back in to have the plates removed from my femurs. The rationale was that if they remained in, if I ever had another problem, the bone could have grown over the screws/plates and they would be unable to repair me as easily. The plate in my wrist, and the bolts in my ankle, knee and shoulder would remain.

They promised it would be only two days or so in hospital – slice down the outside of the legs, unscrew the 24 screws, remove plates, sew me up again and send me home. It sounded OK, but having come this far, I deferred until the licence had arrived and I had been able to take Jean for her first flight at the end of November.

Not Again!

It was a wise decision because two days after I returned home from this latest operation, Jean was taking Chalkie (our West Highland Terrier) around the block when I went for a seat in the smallest room in the house. Arising a few moments later, there was a crack as my right femur snapped, and as I fell back onto the seat, my left femur broke as it hit the woodwork.

When I had had the accident, I had no idea of pain as I was out of it and drugged up for so long. But this really hurt! I clung onto the seat to stop my falling on what was left of my legs and awaited Jean's return. Once she had discovered why I was hiding in the toilet and hysterics dealt with, she called the ambulance. In retrospect, what followed was quite amusing.

Before the ambulance arrived, my GP had heard the call on his radio, and knowing my history and being close by, came to help. Whilst the paramedics arrived, he was feeding me gas and air to relieve the pain, the mask and pipe pushed through a gap in the door – which opened inwards and therefore could not be opened as it was pressing against my legs.

The door needed to come off, so the Fire Brigade were called. They made short work of it, but before they had finished, the local Police who had heard all this on their radio, also came to see what was happening. We lived in a small cul-de-sac. With doctor's car, ambulance, fire engine and police car filling the road, all the neighbours came out to see the action. Just in time for me to be stretchered out screaming and with my trousers round my ankles.

What followed was three weeks of traction, as the legs needed to heal somewhat from the previous operation before the surgeons would go in again. With just one break in each leg, and plates and screws not being an option, they inserted AO Nails into each femur. These are hollow tubes with a gap down one side. In my case each was 44cm long and about 1.3cm wide. These are hammered down the centre of the bone through the head of the femur (and through one's backside), into the space occupied by bone marrow. They have a small thread in the open end at the top to assist pulling them out later.

Three months later, I was walking again, and fit enough to fly. The Rand was probably going to take five years to build and having nearly lost everything again, I was determined to fly now and often, and I needed my own aeroplane now! Fortunately, the school at Conington had a Cessna 172 they wanted to sell to a member on a leaseback arrangement. I checked out in it with instructor John Ditmas, and he demonstrated that he could take off, fly a whole circuit and land without touching the yoke. The aircraft was so stable that he just used rudder and trim. I made an offer, duly accepted.

The Joys of Aircraft Ownership and Leaseback

We still did not have much money, so a loan was necessary to finance the purchase. Jean had spent so much time caring for me (and pushing a wheelchair), that her company had offered her voluntary redundancy, which gave us a deposit. What is more it made her officially unemployed, and at the time there existed something called the "Government Enterprise Allowance Scheme." This was a system by which if you started your own business and therefore came off the unemployed list, they would pay you £40 per week for the first two years. Naturally, Jeanair was immediately formed – a partnership of Jean and I – with immediate registration for VAT so we could get relief for the purchase.

As a partnership we could offset interest on the loan, and book all necessary expenses such as maintenance, replacement radios to bring it up to a reasonable standard etc. This was all good so long as we could make a profit for it to be offset against. The deal with the Flying Club (not the present one at Conington) was they would rent out to members, and we would receive 10%, which was helpful when we did not need the aircraft ourselves.

The downside was that maintenance had to be done at Conington – nowhere else was allowed – and the current engineer enjoyed replacing parts at the drop of a hat. It seemed the Cessna was inside the workshop more than it was outside. It was not a bad aircraft, but it only took something like a hirer to comment that the needle of the ADF was wandering a lot (he had flown past a cumulonimbus cloud) and it would have a couple of hours investigation with corresponding expense.

What was more, as a hire aircraft, many of the users just did not care about how they left it. As an example, I remember finding one of the radio knobs on the floor of the aircraft. Someone could not be ****d to pick it up after they had pulled it off and dropped it.

The other niggle was that the club booked out the aircraft to whoever wanted it without referring to me, so often I could not get it for myself. A prime example was when I wanted to attend my first Jersey Air Rally, and it was already booked. Fortunately, Alan Walton (previously mentioned as learning at same time as myself) offered to share his Cherokee, and we had a great time, and with his wife Eileen and my Jean both being northern girls, we all struck up a long-lasting friendship – and started my lifelong love of air rallies. The same situation occurred for that year's Guernsey Rally and again we shared Alan's Cherokee.

I put up with the Conington situation for nearly eighteen months, carefully weighing up which of the regular hirers were decent people and planning my next move. The move came when the C of A needed renewal. I knew if it was done at Peterborough, it would cost a small fortune (that I didn't have), but I had also learnt that there was an economical engineer at nearby Little Staughton. After consultation with Colton Aviation and my favourite hirers, I had the C of A done there.

A few days later I had a call from Richard, the engineer at Conington, to remind me that the C of A needed doing, and I needed to book his services. I told him it had already been done and he went apoplectic. A few minutes later I had another call, now from the airfield manager (a shoe salesman that had married the boss's daughter) demanding I go to see him. In the resulting meeting, he ordered me and aircraft off the airfield immediately. I declined telling him I was unable to fly as I had just had a drink at lunchtime, but that I would remove the aircraft tomorrow.

Granite City

Eddie Comber and I were due to leave the following day anyway, on our way to Aberdeen to the Granite City Rally, and it was arranged that when we returned, we would fly back to Little Staughton where the aircraft would now be based (alongside the cheaper maintenance organisation – and with cheaper parking fees).

Earlier in the year, I had advanced myself by gaining an IMC rating, which I had done by having 3-day ground school at Oxford with the professionals' tutors there, and then doing the flying with an English instructor based in Portugal at Faro. In those days, Faro had no radar and the only instrument approaches were a VOR/DME and simulated SRAs provided by the instructor. Despite that, I learned well (it was in a 172) and had some amazing days flying. A highlight was the cross-country to Gibraltar, followed by a PAR approach. Jean sat in the rear seat watching Spain go by, and then out over the sea (as you had to do because of the arguments between Spain and UK/Gibraltar). I saw nothing except the instruments through "foggles" until I was told to take them off just before touchdown, when I could see the enormous rock next to the runway.

The training (including theory of approaches I had never practised) was going to be important on our return from Aberdeen.

The day before my test with Eric the examiner, Craig was putting me through my final revision on an atrocious flying day. Surrounded by CBs we were bouncing all over sky.

A BA 737 captain who did have radar was helpfully advising where the storm cells were. On the final approach we were way out of recommended crosswind limits, and Craig told me to keep flying until I could not cope, then he would take over. I was determined to manage it and with rain so hard that it was coming in at the top of the windscreen, I nailed the VOR approach and managed an absolute greaser of a landing. Not a word of praise for me, but Craig turned round to Jean (still in the back seat) and told her how well she had done. My wife is a qualified IMC passenger.

The IMC (to later become the IR/R) was simply the most liberating qualification. No longer so dependent on fair days, it allowed us to go so much further, and we did the last ever Scottish International Air Rally at Edinburgh (Jean and Eileen's highlight was an outdoor serenade on bagpipes by a lone piper, whilst mine was best newcomer award). Eddie and I later flew to the Belfast Rally at Newtownards, and the next day we rallyists flew to a picnic at Enniskillen – a lovely spot. We could hardly believe when the place was so cruelly blown up by the IRA later that year.

But then came Granite City. I had managed a further nine hours or so of instrument flying (including an hour and a half on the way) before reaching Aberdeen. It was the first time they held the rally and had lots of components that were popular in those days – flight planning, timed arrival, longest flight etc. and we did rather well. We had planned to leave early Sunday, but latecomers were still arriving, and we hung on for the final prizegiving. The guest of honour, Bob Pooley, eventually gave us the BA Trophy, and then proceeded to cadge a lift home. He wanted to get to Cranfield but would be happy to take a taxi from Little Staughton.

We had planned with early morning weather but by the time we left it was after 12.30. Our planned time to Bedfordshire gave us ample reserves and the weather had promised fine conditions and light winds. We cruised along on top, well-leaned at FL75, hardly noticing our reducing groundspeed the further south we flew. Getting closer to our new home, we thought about descent, but lo and behold, no holes! It was Sunday afternoon and RAF radar around us started closing down. Fortunately, RAF Wittering was working and when we could not make a cloud break, raised Cranfield on the landline to make sure ILS was available. We turned for Charlie Fox Delta, whilst Wittering gave us radar coverage. I just could not understand why it was taking so long to reach the beacon. I used my Vortrack to make crosscuts and yes, we were on track, but it was taking forever. Not surprising as we now had a 35-knot headwind. It was now after four o'clock.

We finally started our crawl down the glide slope. The aircraft attitude did not move the fuel gauges off zero. The adrenaline had kicked in a long time ago and my focus had never been better (it also kept me awake for about two days afterwards). We broke cloud at minimums and put it down on a windswept, sodden Cranfield. We parked and walked away after a flight lasting 4 hr 20 min. I did not refuel until the next day, when Rogers Aviation managed to squeeze just over 29 gallons into our 31-gallon tanks.

Bob Pooley had wanted to go to Cranfield anyway, had remained calm throughout (and continually offered us boiled sweets all the way) but was definitely grateful to be down and subsequently invited me to his garden party, and eventually to join GAPAN. I never told him that by the time we landed I only had 130 hours in command, and it was my first-ever ILS………

New Arrangements

Having made it safely back to Bedfordshire, I recruited my favourite hirers from Conington to form a group of sorts around the aircraft. These included Eddie of course. Basically, in return for them paying an up-front payment for their share of the insurance, they could fly for a set maintenance cost and the fuel they burned – effectively an early version of the non-equity groups that exist today. This meant a pool of six pilots including myself, who all cared about the aircraft. We had good availability and yet the aircraft got good usage and associated lower maintenance costs per hour. Insurance was still expensive, and it was not until much later when I started shopping around that I discovered that the original insurers (recommended by Conington's manager) were commissioning him every time I renewed. Bloody shoe salesman!

The first year was perfect utilisation at 150 hours between annuals, next 200 hours (the peak), then 160 hours as members of the group moved away due work. We had all benefitted from lower costs and enjoyed sharing aircraft and company, but towards the end my flying was a much bigger percentage of her use.

Jeanair still existed and invoiced the group members as necessary. Unsurprisingly, there were no profits being made, as I was flying them off, and then came a query from the VAT authorities. It seemed obvious to them that it was not a real business – I was just doing this to make my flying cheaper. I had to rapidly convince them otherwise and became a distributor for Vortrack (navigation equipment invented by Gordon Wansborough-White) and then an importer for pilot cases that I advertised in Pilot Magazine. These sold singly at a few a month, but really came into their own when I got the contract to supply Oxford in bulk. Thirty cases a time to be issued to each intake of commercial students. I was in danger of making a profit so had to fly more to use it up (on promotional visits to sell cases to flying clubs around the country, of course).

Each year, the accumulated losses were carried forward by my accountant. But by now, my day job was starting to really pay significant profits, and we discovered a wrinkle in the HMRC rules. It has changed now, but in those days, if you had more than one business, you could offset any losses on one against profits of the other. The accumulated and ongoing losses of Jeanair meant I paid little income tax for many years, despite earning well.

Further Skills

Shortly after I finally got my licence, I had been nominated for the AOPA Award for Individual Merit – which I won due to my perseverance in continuing training despite injuries. It was a nice piece of silverware, and the Scottish International had added another to the trophy table.

The 1980s and 1990s were probably the heyday of Air Rallies, and I discovered they were one of my favourite ways to spend even more money on aviation. Having been introduced to them by Alan Walton (Jersey and Guernsey in his Cherokee) we set about finding as many new ones to attend as we could manage.

Each rally was different. Most had the usual elements of planning and equipment to be carried to be marked (which all taught you to be a better pilot), log-keeping, timed arrivals, spot landings, navigation exercises, and concours d'elegance competitions. I tasted a few minor successes but was surprised how some participants did not really bother to compete, and it was obvious there were some nice trophies to be had if you put in a little work.

By then, Alan had become an instructor and worked at Earls Colne at weekends (he would later become an examiner too). As I no longer flew with a club after leaving Conington, I joined in with their team efforts. We would field teams of up to six or seven aircraft and were really quite organised. After gaining experience, my first major overall win was the Jersey Rally in 1988.

What was even sweeter, was that I could stay on the island for a few days after, doing my day job of visiting architects and contractors, before hopping over to Guernsey to do the same – and all my expenses were chargeable.

Precision

It was not long after this first big win, that I saw an advert for the British Precision Pilots Association. They were recruiting new blood with the prospects of taking part in the World Air Rally Championships which in 1988 were to take place at Northampton (Sywell). Eddie and I decided we would have a go at the elimination trials and duly went to Finmere to compete. We were rubbish.

The World Air Rally Championship is not a "gin & tonic" rally like those we knew. It is very precise, accurate track-keeping and timing, coupled with observation of targets that you can see – but only if you keep superbly close to track, and you must know precisely where you are so you can annotate them on your chart. More than a few seconds out at turning points and you have no chance.

Whereas planning for a Precision Competition (flown solo) is done before you go to the aircraft (and is marked), for a Rally team of two, the co-ordinates of the route are only handed to you in the aircraft about twenty minutes before your allotted take-off time, and the navigator needs to plot furiously in the cockpit. You use at least two maps so that when you run out of time the first map goes to the pilot to take off and fly the legs plotted so far, whilst the navigator continues plotting the next. Maps are exchanged regularly as turning points run out.

All of this is done without being allowed to use any electronic devices. You use a whizz-wheel, protractor, ruler, stopwatch. No radio navigation is allowed – in fact, everything is covered up and sealed so you cannot use them – unless completely lost - then you can do whatever is necessary such as breaking the seals to get home safely and be disqualified.

When you have made a complete mess of the course, and are exhausted, you have the pleasure of a spot landing.

This is better than in a Precision Flying competition, where you are solo, and there are four to be done. The first is a "normal" where you are permitted to use power and flaps. Second is a glide, but flaps are allowed. Third is a flapless glide, followed by the fourth "obstacle". For this last one, you can use power and flaps, but you must land over a line of bunting two metres high and fifty metres before the line – which believe me, is quite off-putting.

(At a BPPA event held at Beccles I did manage to pull the bunting out and drag it down the runway with my undercarriage, but it was the only time. I made up for my sins that day by talking down a newly qualified lady pilot who had taken her parents for a jolly immediately after gaining her licence. Unused to a 172 she could not get approach speed right and after several attempts she needed calming down, and as a fellow 172 pilot I could talk her through it).

Effectively you are training for a precautionary landing, an engine failure, an engine and electrics failure, and a precautionary landing into a short field (where you must land over the hedge/wall as short as you can). Judging is done by other competitors and supporters positioning themselves at ten metre intervals before and after the line. The "box" is from thirty metres before the line, to fifty metres after. Five penalty points are awarded for every metre before the line, and three points for every metre after the line. The first metre after the line scores zero penalties. Outside the box is maximum penalties.

Because of the danger to the judges stood by the ten metres markers, you must roll out of the box before applying power and taking off again for the next discipline (or gain more penalties). You only get one attempt at each. There are lots of other ways to attract penalties – abnormal landing (nose-wheel first), bouncing etc. It is quite amazing how many points you can accrue, and whenever I subsequently took part in precision competitions, I did!

Finmere attempts had been made in June. We were one of seven teams assessed to be whittled down to five for the August championship. Whilst waiting for news, I did the GNAV competition at White Waltham (later to be rebranded TOPNAV) and won the Airtour Sword and £100. Then I heard that two other teams had dropped out of the running for Sywell. By default, Eddie and I would represent Great Britain!

One of our group members, Dave Moreau, was a journalist and with an eye on his fees, wrote an article about the "bionic pilot" who had been bolted together after surviving a horrific accident and was now to fly for Britain. I had never been a self-publicist, but he included a paragraph about looking for sponsors which I thought justified it. Along with an article about a Mr Arnold Glass who had just bought six English Electric Lightnings and parked them at Cranfield, it filled a complete page of the Sunday Express - which in those days was a broadsheet newspaper. This was to result in a more amusing/annoying article later.

World Champions - not us!

The event arrived too soon. We had only had one further practice before positioning the aircraft at Sywell. The BPPA organisers had rapidly issued us with our team uniforms emblazoned with "Great Britain Flying Team" – which of course we had to pay for. All expenses were our own, unlike the Polish Team who were government sponsored with everything paid for, and nearly always cleaned up the medals. Similarly, the French got lots of cash for practice flying and continue to be a leading team, now that Poland is no longer sponsored.

Teams came from all over Europe, and even some from South Africa & South America. Never having taken part in something like this we were very impressed with the camaraderie between the competing teams. They nearly all knew each other but welcomed us as new boys. Under the auspices of the FAI, there was a great deal of ceremony at opening and close, and in between a practice day, then two long competition days.

The first competition course was three hours to Haverfordwest (and then two and a half hours back). Next day's two and a half hours started and finished at Sywell. Because the three competitions had been completed without weather problems, we had a free day and flew into Keyston, a nearby uphill strip that led to the Pheasant pub for an excellent lunch. By the time we got back, results were being announced and we unsurprisingly came very close to bottom.

But we were not last. There were others worse than us, and below them the Italians, who had been caught cheating, were disqualified. One of their team members was caught sat in his cockpit talking to the others by radio and advising target locations. When challenged they said it was their duty to win at all costs.

In five days, we had flown some 12 hours and were quite exhausted, but had had a wonderful time, and decided we would continue with Precision Flying at least.

But something strange had happened each day. Each evening I would get a message from the hotel that someone I had never heard of had called me and could I ring them back? Because it was necessary to attend team briefings, I never had chance until the final evening. When I finally connected, the gentleman (I use the term loosely) told me he wanted to do a further newspaper article in an effort to gain me sponsorship, and quizzed me about my flying, my accident and my current health. He promised I would see something in due course.

I had never heard of the paper he mentioned, but the following week I was chatting to a customer (a buyer for Hilton Hotels) who was an aviation enthusiast and had seen the Sunday Express article and I mentioned that another item should come out soon. When I told him, it would be in a sporting publication, called the Sunday Sport, he broke into laughter. Unbeknown to me, it was a rag that featured made-up stories sometimes based on a little truth. Apparently, it once featured a headline "B-17 bomber found on Moon". If only I had known I would never have spoken to the man.

In due course, the edition was published and there I was. Pictures gleaned from other (local) newspapers showed me, my wrecked car, even the x-rays of metalwork in my legs. But it was the headline that appalled me. "STEELY LOVER DRIVES WIFE NUTS IN BED" it proclaimed. It then described in detail about how the metalwork creaked at inappropriate moments and needed lubrication. The only truth in the whole article, was the last line "Martin has now returned to the sport he loves, flying".

Embarrassed and incensed (about equally) I would have sued but discovered that the reason he kept phoning me is that if a conversation had been had, it was his word against mine about what had been said. I had no chance of success and promised Jean that I would never again talk to a reporter about anything, good or bad. Thankfully, no-one we knew bought the rag, and I kept very quiet about the article until now, but it's more than thirty years ago, and I can laugh about it.

More Gin & Tonic

The day following our return from Sywell, we were on the way to Granite City for our second try, and we won outright. A month later, Jean replaced Eddie, and we did our first in France, the Stanton Rally at Angers. From there we left for La Rochelle, then hopped around the French islands and then on the way back did the spot-landing competition at Cherbourg before more "work" on the Channel Islands to cover expenses. This self-employed lark made things very manageable.

Jean had a taste for the Jersey/Guernsey type of rally, where there was good social activity, with dining, dancing and at both venues fancy dress. This seems to be a thing on the Channel Islands – presumably because everyone knows everyone else so well, they feel the need to look different on a regular basis.

With our friends from Earls Colne, we made efforts to join in, and over the years we have been French waiters (receiving suitable glares from the real ones at Jersey), the Flintstones, and at one we were representing aircraft. With suitable patches painted onto long johns and vest, large floppy ears, and an enormous nappy from which a tail protruded, I was a Beagle Pup. It was so effective that when I had to visit the gents later in the evening, I was followed by several people to see how I would cope.

A mixture of serious competitions (BPPA) and social rallies became the norm. Skills learned from the BPPA stood me in good stead for the less serious, as by using techniques such as minute marks, timed arrivals were easy to manage, and navigation was easy with the correct chart procedures.

And the landings practice was regular and prepared you for not just the more ordinary competitions, but if needed would help in an emergency.

Necessary Painting

When I had bought Delta India, although a sound aeroplane, she was not pretty. When new in 1969 she had been painted in solid post office red (but dull) – everything except the wings which were white. The flying club at Conington had tried to brighten her up by adding stripes and over-painting the top of the cowling and fuselage, tailplane, and fin/rudder. Unfortunately, they used cream rather than white. Very amateur.

One of the club members who hired her had flown through a hailstorm which peppered the tailplane and chipped off random cream paint. With the original paint now showing it looked like red rust spots breaking through.

Then as I flew one day, there was suddenly a slick of blood across the windscreen. My propellor had cut the head off a sparrow, the body of which hit my cowling and cracked the fibreglass as it entered the engine compartment, before ending up on a rear cylinder and being well cooked. Only a little thing but travelling at 100mph the damage was significant (although not quite as bad as the buzzard I hit some years later). Repairs and paint were needed, so why not the whole aircraft?

Little Staughton was home to one of the best paint shops in the country. Fred (now retired to his villa on the continent) had a superb reputation and being based there, the decision was easy. But what scheme and what colours?

When I had learnt at Conington, a fellow student was the really nice, very tall, Stuart Miller. Stuart had qualified and spent the next five years building a Bolkow Junior in his garage. He was an artist and when it came to schemes and paint his blue aircraft with gold stars (designed by himself) was a sight to behold. I admired the aircraft but could not understand why he had built a single-seater – but that mattered not to him as his long hours in the garage had also gained him a divorce.

I commissioned Stuart to design me a scheme, which Fred then implemented. It was a turning point for my rallying, as I not only did well in navigation but started winning concours d'elegance competitions too. Stuart was a PFA pilot, strictly VFR, and when I took him for his reward flight and we climbed through cloud, he was terrified!

What was nice about Concours competitions, was that rather than silverware loaned for the year, often it was beautifully engraved glassware that you kept forever. This was a favourite with Jean as it did not require polishing and could be used for floral displays etc. But on one occasion I really blotted my copybook. Having won the Jersey Rally, along with the loan silverware I had received a presentation box filled with a decanter and six sherry glasses, all engraved with the Jersey Aero Club crest.

After a heavy night, the following morning I picked it up and as I only had hold of the lid, the box itself fell to the floor and only one sherry glass and the decanter's stopper were unbroken. My popularity with Jean had waned again.

AOPA

I had joined the Aircraft Owners and Pilots Association very shortly after qualifying. It seemed a good idea to have an organisation batting on our behalf, even if subscriptions were expensive, and the award they had given me had been a welcome surprise.

I never needed their assistance, but it was good to know that if I found myself in trouble they could be called on for advice, and I enjoyed their magazine along with all the others I purchased.

With a two-year membership and for a few pounds extra, I bought their "Aircrew Card". It is a simple ID card with name, photograph, licence number etcetera, which is really handy at major airports when security demands ID to get airside. But a nice touch on the back is a note to "Hotel Operators: The holder of this card is a licensed pilot and/or aircraft owner engaged in International Air Transport. Please grant normal AIR CREW courtesy discounts. Thank you". It is a magic little card. If hotels have vacant rooms, they much prefer to fill them at a low price and then be able to provide food and drink that they can make money on, rather than leave them empty. The card gives them a good excuse to help!

One needs to make a polite enquiry at reception as to whether industry rates are available and proffer the card (and it is a good idea to mention you will really need a meal and a good bottle of wine). On many occasions when I did this, they had never seen the card before, but it did not prevent them helping. I believe my best deal achieved was a Hilton double room for £10. It all helps to pay the membership.

In 2003 AOPA asked all pilots to go flying on the 100th anniversary of the first flight and not needing any excuse to get airborne, I did.

The same year, they introduced their AOPA Wings scheme. Several organisations have similar schemes, but theirs was the first approved under the CAA PROUD initiative. The CAA must have worked hard to come up with that acronym, as it stands for Pilot Recognition for Operational Up-skilling and Development. Anyone who is newly qualified as a pilot, private or commercial, can apply for their bronze wings, at no cost and they do not have to be a member of AOPA.

You can then move up through silver, gold and to platinum with a selection of minimum flight times, achievements, seminar attendances and air touring experience. You need a mixture of improvements to your flying, whether upgrades to your qualifications or additional ratings, further training of just about any sort, and taking part in fun events like navigation or air racing competitions, along with seminars such as safety days. At the platinum level the air touring experience needs to include one flight of 450nm and that can include overnight stops etc.

As you progress you receive a discreet set of metal wings (framing the AOPA shield) to pin to whatever you wish, and these are appropriate colours. What is more, they are all free to AOPA members and only £10 to non-members (after the bronze which is free to all). I was very happy to calculate that I qualified for platinum as soon as the scheme was launched, and therefore saved them the cost of three sets of wings on the way. I cannot remember the CEO, Martin Robinson, thanking me for it, but I am sure he would have.

The scheme is a great way to keep making progress. Too often flying can become just a route to a £100 hamburger, and we did not do all that work learning just for that.

Would You fly a 172 to UK from Wichita?

Unfortunately, no-one asked me to do this, but the dealer at Wycombe Air Park ran a competition at the London Air Show where you had to estimate the flying time that it would take to do so. Having guessed the route and making some rough calculations, I seem to remember I came up with 51.5 hours.

This was nearer than anyone else and later that year I received my prize of an hour's free flying in a brand-new 172SP G-PLBI. Considerably plusher than my trusted steed, and more powerful but with an appropriate price. Delta India would have to remain, but I would address the power issue later.

I think the London Air Show (which was an indoor exhibition) only happened once, but it did give me chance to land a British Airways 737 on their simulator. I still have the print-out showing my track and glide path. It was good enough that I could have walked away from the landing.

Work and its Contribution

With almost fixed "sunk costs" of an aeroplane, the more you fly the cheaper it gets (that is the theory). But if you can use it for work and get costs covered, why wouldn't you?

I received a call about an architect in Canterbury that was having problems with our material. The only way to understand what had happened was to visit the site in Canterbury and it was urgent. Workmen were stopped and waiting on site for my visit. A quick check and there was an airfield just outside Canterbury, to the west and just north of the A2, so after the necessary phone calls to arrange permission and taxi, off I went.

"Airfield" was a very loose description. It was a narrow strip of gravel laid on a hill. The bottom of the gravel was inside a forest, and at the top was a small plateau with a portacabin. The southerly wind meant an upward landing, so I sunk down between the trees and then powered up the slope until it was safe to stop.

The taxi managed to find its way into the woods, and I went and did my job. The architect was duly impressed by my flying visit. Back at the strip, the operator and his friend had arrived, and were interested in the performance of a Cessna (they had a rather old Cherokee – the only aircraft there). As a thank-you for use of the strip, I gave them a short jolly with downhill take-off and uphill landing, before departing back to Little Staughton.

Quite some time later I wanted to visit Canterbury with Jean and I could tell she was nervous as we descended into the trees. I was made to understand that I should never, ever land there again.

And I never did, because after a few beers, the Cherokee owner took off uphill and having just managed to clear the A2, he wallowed into the trees on the opposite side of the road. The aircraft was written off, he was prosecuted, and the airfield was closed forever. It is still there (I look whenever passing) and if the donkey stops, I will use it.

Mr Bob Pooley's Garden Party and Return

As mentioned before, I had a new friend in Robert Pooley. He invited me to his house where he proceeded to load me up with just about every flight guide his company had produced, and all manner of aviation accessories and maps.

We were then invited to land at White Waltham and attend the garden party that he was putting on for the Guild of Air Pilots and Navigators (of whom he was Grand Master). There was a spot landing competition too, but the real entertainment was in his garden, with hot air balloons, aerobatic displays, the RAF band, and even Charles Shea-Simonds parachuting in from a Tiger Moth.

It was a fabulous day, and we were about to land back at Little Staughton just before 18.00. The airfield is completely uncontrolled and is only used by a few residents and a maintenance base, all of which were absent at that time on a Sunday.

On very short finals for 07, I suddenly glimpsed an aircraft coming towards us intent on landing downwind. Power on and I went around and landed off the next circuit. By then the Trinidad had landed and pulled into some hard standing on the side of the runway. A girl was sat in the cockpit whilst the pilot was unloading large red, white, and blue trolley bags (as used in supermarket carts on the continent). I slowed to a stop alongside him and asked what was happening and did he need any help? Apparently, he had had a "fuel problem" and had to land, but it was fixed now. I did not believe a word of it and taxied away to park the aircraft.

Once safely parked I wanted to know what was really happening and started to drive towards the runway. At that moment, the Trinidad took off. Before I reached the runway, another chap that I had never seen before, wearing shorts and trainers, appeared in front of me and started asking whether he could get flying lessons here. As he spoke a Datsun drove onto the runway and I questioned who it was. "It's just my brother, he wants to see how long the runway is". By the time I had got him out of the way and was approaching the place where the Trinidad had parked, the Datsun driver was throwing the last trolley bag into the hatchback and sped off, leaving the other guy by the taxiway. We gave chase.

Whilst rushing through nearby villages we attempted to tell the police what was happening via my early-model mobile phone, and I think they had trouble believing what we were telling them. The pace had picked up and there were kids on bikes and horses, and I realised this could be dangerous, so told the police the registration number of the vehicle and the aircraft and said we would back off. They agreed to meet us back at the airfield to take statements. We were still waiting for them when the Datsun reappeared, saw us, and sped off again. For the second time we started after them, but then they started slowing down and signalling us to go past. If this were drugs, they could be dangerous people and I declined and returned to the airfield.

We were relating the story to the police when they got a radio call that a chap in shorts and trainers had been detained in nearby Great Staughton, and could we go and identify him? They whisked us round there in the squad car, and it was not him. But as we sat in the car, the real shorts and trainers walked past bold as brass and Jean cried "that's him!". With him promptly nicked, we returned to the airfield to finish the story then secure the aircraft.

The Datsun driver was caught a little later when he attempted a further return to collect his brother, not knowing he was at Bedford Police Station by now. A

Sergeant (who was acting Inspector that day) saw him in his rear-view mirror and pulled across the road to stop him.

It took longer to find the aircraft's pilot. He had filed a flight plan from Brussels to Birmingham, dropping into Little Staughton to leave his load. Once he had cleared customs at Birmingham, he went home to his base at Elstree. It was three in the morning before he was knocked-up (and then locked up) by the police. He had a lot of explaining to do, not least to his wife about who the girl in the cockpit was (they had been in Brussels together over the weekend).

I had been wrong in thinking it was drugs. It was only rolling tobacco and they were evading a significant amount of duty (it transpired later to be about £3600) but who knows whether if successful they would have tried something more serious? Trinidad and Datsun were confiscated, and they were allowed to re-purchase them after they had paid their fines of £1500 each. As far as I was concerned their major offence was endangering Jean and I by landing against us, and then thinking we were stupid enough to believe them.

It seems the police were more than impressed with the idea of capturing airborne smugglers. In the following weeks, we received a letter of thanks and were invited to the opening of a new police station, then to a presentation by HM Collector of Taxes, where we were given an inscribed decanter from the Customs Investigation Unit. And then we were featured in Portcullis, the internal journal of HMRC – fortunately, what their reporter said was true.

Good Job I had Practiced

Only a month after the smuggling incident, I made an early start, leaving Staughton to fly to Southampton to do some work. Sometime into the flight, my rev counter needle started wandering up and down. The engine was running smoothly and the only thought I had was that the cable could be fraying and snagging. I flew on a little further considering my options.

If it was just the instrument or cable, then it was safe to continue, but when I was ready to return from Southampton, I would be unable to do an accurate power check before take-off. Discretion being the better part of valour, I decided to turn around and see my engineer at Staughton to fix it. Shortly after that, the needle went to zero and stayed there. The Continental O-300D engine was still running smoothly, and temperature and pressures were all normal. But as I steered towards home, I was preparing myself if it was something more.

I had told Luton ATC I was returning home with an instrument problem and as I was nearing the MoD station at Bedford, they told me they had phoned them and although they were not open yet, they would work me, and I changed frequency. I had just called them with my registration when there was an enormous clonk and the propellor in front of me froze. No windmilling – the engine had seized. Whilst there is a standard format for a Mayday call, I simply said "Ah, engine stopped" to which Bedford replied "Cleared land any runway you can make" which still sounded challenging as I was four and a half miles away and only at 2500 feet.

BPPA training kicked in and best glide speed was achieved. I had a tailwind on my side, and even needed flap to get in. I think the frozen prop caused less drag and helped. As I coasted to a stop, the MoD fire engines came in from either side and followed me. Taxying was going to be a problem, so once assured there was no fire to be dealt with, they pushed me into a hangar to await a rebuilt engine.

What had gone wrong? After research I discovered that there was a square lug at the end of the camshaft that drove the oil pressure pump and subsequently the rev counter. Some camshafts had been made of softer metal than needed and there was an Airworthiness Directive to check for any excess play every 100 hours. My engineer had missed it. When the rev counter had started to oscillate, it was the corners being knocked off the square, and when it went to zero it was round and no longer driving anything. At that moment I had still had oil pressure and temperature, but that did not last – and hence seizure.

Norvic Engines agreed to build me a new engine at great expense, but to save the core charge, I had to supply them with a serviceable crankcase and camshaft, and my camshaft certainly was not serviceable – it was "blue". I had to purchase another second-hand camshaft and pay for it to be reground to tolerances – in all I shelled out £1500 to save the £3000 core charge. Damn good job it was an expense I could offset to Jeanair and then my real job, as well as the enormously expensive replacement engine.

Marking Time for a New Start

Norvic were remarkably quick, and I was flying again in just 50 days. But nearly two months is still a long time, and my good friend Alan had read of the drama in the local paper and knew I would be having withdrawal symptoms.

By then he had swapped his ex-Hamble Cherokee for a sporty little Robin – the aerobatic R2160D. He was still instructing at Earls Colne and made me an offer I could not refuse. I would meet him at Conington. He would check me out on the aircraft (I had flown it once before, but only briefly) as I flew him to Earls Colne. If I was good enough, he would sign me off and I could take it away for the day to play with, as long as I replaced the Avgas and remembered to collect him at the end of the day.

On arrival at EGSR, he dismounted and told me to go off. "How much can I do?" "As much as you like as long as you fill her up" was his answer. He may have regretted saying that as the delightful aircraft flew for 6.9 hours that day! That tided me over until Delta India was back and available.

A new engine needed flying hard and fast to break in the cylinders, so some decent long flights took me to Newcastle, Blackpool and then over to Angers again for a second go at the Stanton Rally. The pilot organiser of this had tourist property there, and with accommodation, steam train rides, and lunch on a riverboat it was another entertaining weekend, and the Navex and Spot Landing Trophy joined the others in the cabinet.

Only three weeks later it was Guernsey again, and I not only won the overall rally but £300 as a prize. I was beginning to like this!

Geoff Jones had previously asked me to write something about rallying, and it had been published in Flyer Magazine – again there was payment for my flying. I did another write-up about rallying and it appeared in the now-defunct Pilots International magazine. Armed with these articles and others I had written for AOPA, I approached the people at Stallion 51 in Florida. I had read about Crazy Horse, their TF-51 Mustang, and could I come and fly and write about it?

A deal was struck and during my November holiday we flew from Orlando Executive, where they were temporarily based. My host Lee Lauderbach has probably the highest hours on a Mustang anywhere – the wartime pilots would have had far fewer. He performed some superb aerobatics and let me follow through and then repeat, rolls, barrel rolls, even a loop. To a lowly Cessna pilot, there was somewhat of a difference in performance!

The subsequent article "Mustang Flying in Florida!" appeared in Pilots International, and since then I have read virtually the same article written by others at about six or seven-year intervals. Eventually I was paid by John Olsson, who ran the magazine and needed chasing, and it more than covered the fuel contribution I had made to Lee. I determined that one day I wanted to fly a Spitfire.

Note: Many years later I bumped into Lee at the Sun and Fun Convention in Florida. By then he now owned two TF-51s – Crazy Horse 1 & 2. After reintroducing myself I was invited into the Stallion 51 marquee overlooking the display line, where I was treated to lunch and could watch Lee perform his magic aerobatics again. It reinforced that the Mustang is definitely my favourite, but I still wanted to fly the Spitfire so I could compare.

More Maintenance

Most mature readers will remember the famous Michael Fish "There won't be a hurricane" gaffe in 1987, which was followed by devastation of southern counties' forests. But they might not remember there was a second storm that qualified as a hurricane just three years later.

When the first one struck, Delta India escaped unharmed, although a Cessna 150 in front of her lifted off and landed on top of the Rockwell Commander parked alongside my aircraft. There but for the grace of God….

Just two months after the new engine had been fitted following seizure, the second hurricane struck in the early hours. She was parked in a different spot on her own, secured by screw-in tie-downs, which were ripped out by the lift she experienced. Rocking from wingtip to wingtip, both wing's outer spars were bent upwards, their aluminium skins were torn, and both fibreglass wingtips destroyed.

Surprisingly, this is not uncommon storm damage, so Cessna have a standard repair kit for the spars, and that was ordered quickly. I was horrified at how much new fibreglass tips would cost from Cessna and had read about Madras Supertips that could be fitted under an STC. With a significant droop below the wing, these were claimed to either allow you to fly faster for the same fuel or use less fuel at regular cruise speeds. Importantly a pair cost much less than a single tip from Cessna. They also looked great!

I checked with the local CAA surveyor, and he saw no problem, so I contacted Mr Ace Demers of Madras Air Services and ordered the correct ones for a 172H.

My day job at the time was selling a lot of wallcoverings imported from USA, so I had a pet freight company that did a lot of work for us and were happy to include them in an import shipment for free.

Duly fitted, my engineer applied for the promised minor mod to be signed off, but the CAA had a change of mind. They deliberated and decided that the tips would cause a change to the wing-loading and they would need to test-fly the aircraft, which they did. All this came at a cost, and when they finally agreed they could stay, their fees were almost £1000. Moreover, they decided they would have to amend the operating manual to disallow spinning (not that I ever wanted to spin) and because they said the wing-loading meant it should be flown either slower or lighter and as they could not give this option, they reduced the MAUW by 62 Kg.

Whilst they were deliberating, I had kept flying by borrowing a regular pair of tips, so these now came off and the Supertips went back on. On the face of it, the economical tips had cost a fortune, but the reduced all-up weight did not worry me as I had hardly ever filled all the seats. And since then, as the aircraft is now under a tonne, my insurance is cheaper, and where landing fees are by weight, I often save. I believe I have more than broke even over the last thirty years.

As a bonus, the tips are very distinctive, and at nearly every fly-in I meet new people who come to ask about them.

Just Use It

I had a serviceable engine and snazzy new tips. The remainder of the year was spent flying in all directions, not least to Kilkenny to photograph the nearby stately home that my partner had bought. He was still making far too much money compared to me.

Eire was a favourite venue, and I toured as much as I could including out to the Aran Islands – Inishmore, Inishmaan and Inisheer. Before coasting out it was fun to fly beneath the Cliffs of Moher. This was where the Irish had waved goodbye to their families as they sailed to America to avoid the potato famine. American tourists return to the spot to gaze seaward, and it is nice to wave up at them.

My August trip to the Granite City Rally persuaded me that it had really developed into a favourite. That year it even featured a Radio Navex which I have never seen anywhere else, but it was run by ATC, we were tracked by them, and our hold and approaches were judged. The main man was Geoff Greavey, who later used to do the radio at PFA (to become LAA) rallies down south. He was a super chap and we got on well.

Two months later I had need to call him because of a problem at work. One of the contracts my partner company had was to supply wallcovering to TSB branches around the country. It was a special heavy-duty fabric-backed vinyl in a mauve colour. We had it made in USA and they bought thousands of metres.

Now a decorator had installed it in three remote branches and complained it was faulty. My role with my partner's company was to provide technical expertise, and I knew the batch was perfect (we'd sold lots all over the country) but I also knew that if installed incorrectly it could look wrong.

I spoke to the Scottish decorator who expected me to roll over and just send a replacement as the jobs were so remote, and I would not want to travel and view. How wrong he was! A quick call to Geoff and I had an invite to land at the strip at Insch. Geoff would collect me and drive me to the sites at Huntley and Keith, put me up for the night in his bungalow and next day I would fly with him to Wick where the third job was, and we did just that. At each site I was able to prove the decorator was at fault.

As Geoff was an ATCO we booked our arrivals as Radio Navigation Exercises and got free landing fees everywhere. We extended the trip to Inverness, and after I dropped him back at Insch, I visited Glasgow for good measure. By the time I was home, I had had nearly ten hours free flying all paid for by my partner. I had still saved him more than the cost of replacement material.

Changing Arrangements

For the next few years, the group arrangements continued, but the other members were flying less and less and some moved away. I was still doing regular rallies and BPPA competitions and in between getting as many new fields in my logbook as I could, and in those days, it was affordable to land at major airports around the country. I am glad I took that opportunity when I could.

Whilst we did little bits to the Rand homebuilt in Eddie's garage it was really festering there as it was more fun to go flying. Moreover, by now Eddie (and Maggie) had produced three girls, and his focus was shifted. Eventually we gave up and sold the component parts, mainly fibreglass that we had purchased and the Revmaster engine. The wooden fuselage we had built which was on its undercarriage ended up in a hangar in Cambridgeshire. It will never fly. Eventually Eddie had enough time to make a fast-build Jabiru – rather like an Airfix kit you glue the halves together! A great little aeroplane but I could never get over the throttle being between your legs under the seat.

Gradually I was flying more types whenever the opportunity arose. Often this was on the annual holiday, which tended to be Florida because of the variety you could hire and these included Harvard, WACO UPF-7, and even a Piper Cougar. The Cougar was to become my only twin lesson for reasons to be explained later.

My stay at Little Staughton (and the group) was soon to come to an end when I needed to relocate due to changes in the day job. My partner wanted me to transfer into the main company, giving up my self-employed role, and as he would make me a director, I had little choice. It was an ideal time to wrap up the partnership for tax purposes, confirmed by my accountant.

As I would be taking more of an office role, it was necessary to be closer to head office at Banbury, and I managed to buy off-plans a newbuild adjacent to Wellesbourne airfield. It was just outside the ATZ, but often under students' bomber-command size circuits.

Once the house was completed, Delta India moved home too, and the remaining couple of group members handed back their keys. I will always be grateful for the times (and costs) we shared.

Never thought I'd be in the USAF

Whilst waiting for the house to be completed, we were still in Cambridgeshire and the local Hereward Radio was running a charity auction. The prize was a day as Station Commander of RAF Alconbury.

I had just sold the British Gas shares that Mrs Thatcher had made possible and decided that it was a good cause to contribute to, so waited in the wings until the last moment and made a killer bid by phone. It was either too rich or too late, as no-one came back with a better bid, and it was mine. Moreover, whilst I would be Commander for the day, the invitation was for a family of four, all to be shown around the base and wined and dined.

Jean and I were just a couple, so on the day it made sense to introduce Eileen (Alan's wife and Jean's best friend) as her sister, and Alan was therefore the brother-in-law. Luckily, no security checks were made.

It was a remarkable day of entertainment that included being fitted out with my uniform (I got to keep the badges including my name patch showing an A10 Warthog, and all the squadron badges, cap etc). I then signed orders (photo-opportunity) and accepted the flag and command. A tour of the base included a G-suit fitting and test inflation. Hmm – quite uncomfortable. Into the hangars and dispersal and looking at A10s and then lunch. Then it was the tower, where I asked the obvious question. As I was the station commander, it was OK for me to land my Cessna there, wasn't it?

No, it was not, but we struck a deal. I would be allowed to fly an approach. They would talk me down to twenty feet on a PAR, but if I touched rubber, they threatened to shoot me. Once I had handed back uniform and kit, and relinquished command, that is what we did. We went back to Staughton to get Delta India. I donned foggles and with Alan as lookout pilot, we returned to Alconbury.

This was the first PAR I had done since Gibraltar and have to say it went well. Certainly, when the glasses came off, I was in the right place, but had to open up the throttle quickly to avoid their threat. I still wish I had touched and got it in the logbook, but a deal is a deal.

On future occasions they allowed me to practice again, and then we moved. Sometime later I flew over and all the aircraft had gone, and the runways had been turned into a car park (just after they spent £3 million resurfacing it) and now it is being developed for housing. What a waste.

Warwickshire Convenience

The new house we bought in 1991 was in a great place. I could be at the airfield within 5 minutes, and we were only ten minutes from Leamington Spa, Warwick, and Stratford-on-Avon. The house was part of a nice little development built to resemble a farmhouse and converted outbuildings. We were to be in "The Linhay". It was on the site of a previous pig farm, so I am sure no-one objected to the planning application. It was all to be new build.

We were buying from plans which showed a more than generous garden (not football pitch size, yet five a side would work), but just before we were to exchange contracts the man from Berkeley Homes came to see us. He informed us they had found a small inaccuracy, in that a strip of the rear garden to the left (some 10m x 3m) did not actually belong to them but was associated with an older house across the street. Supposedly the owner was not even aware it was his, and once we had signed up for the property, they would approach him and ask him to sell it/sign it over. Meanwhile, we can exchange contracts, can't we?

I argued that the landowner might not want to sell, and I wanted Berkeley to have a real incentive to get it right and we settled on £10,000 reduction in our house price and proceeded. We would never miss it anyway, there would be quite enough lawn to mow.

The real owner of the patch of land had been trying to sell his own house for some time, but having no garden at all, was having trouble. As soon as he was aware he owned the land, even though it was disconnected from his house (which was the other side of the village road), he succeeded and moved away.

Before we moved in, Berkeley had laid the enormous garden to lawn, and it was completely surrounded by a six-foot high tanalised close-boarded fence. We needed a large mower and that meant a large shed, which was erected adjacent to the fence between us and the piece of land we did not own and would obviously never get.

I was in the office at Banbury when Jean called to tell me of an exchange with our new neighbour who owned the strip of land and had moved in six months after us. She had knocked at the front door to inform Jean that her husband would be creosoting their side of *our* fence. "But we don't want it creosoted – it's tanalised and doesn't need it, so don't". The debate continued for a few minutes, and then the neighbour asked whether we would move the shed, as the apex was visible over the top of the fence? "We can't, it's on a concrete base and you can only see three inches of it above the fence, and you can't see it at all from your house".

"You will tell me before you do anything else in your garden, won't you?" asked the neighbour heatedly. Jean's reply was "No I bloody well won't" and shut the front door in her face.

That afternoon I had my first trial lesson with Heli-Air at Wellesbourne. The Robinson R22 hopped across to our village, and we hovered for several minutes checking clearances before landing in our back garden. Many of our friendly neighbours in the new development came out to watch (and later told me they were impressed), but we never again heard from our visitor who lived across the road.

New Clubmates

A new airfield meant new buddies. There were lots, really lots, of flying schools at Wellesbourne. Initially I spent a lot of time with South Warwickshire Flying School who trained RAF cadets each year and made lots of new friends, but my time was split with BPPA Competitions (where I had moved up from Sportsman Class to Open) and rallying with the guys from Earls Colne, and every fly-in and event I could find.

In 1992 we had an invitation to Germany. The Neiderheim Powered Flying Club was an RAF flying club and was based on RAF Laarbruch – they were to run a rally! We gathered the team together at Earls Colne and set off across the oggin. Two and a half hours later we touched down at Laarbruch, where we were wined and dined before being taken by coach to our quarters – which were in Holland! Venlo was only forty minutes away and we were billeted there for economy.

Everything was comprehensively arranged, and we were collected next morning to be returned to the airfield to do the Navex competition (second place achieved) and later that day, flour-bombing (Club Trophy won), and dinner in the Officers Mess.

Coaches again, and the next day was to be a cracker. We were to do a dawn patrol, pitched against the club Slingsby aircraft. Once we were all in the briefing room, it was as if we were in the service. Officers in turn gave us airfield brief, met brief, and mission brief. We were issued maps marked with two "funnels" through which we must fly. The first was quite wide, but the second was not, and we had to pass through both without our registrations being taken by the spotters. From memory they fielded about 4 or 5 Slingsbys.

The only height limit was a maximum 7000 feet at the first funnel, and not below 500 feet anywhere. It would take us 20-30 minutes to pass through both funnels once we were up and ready.

After the officers had left to ready their aircraft, we had a short time to debate how we would try to evade them. The decision was to go in waves of 3 or 4 aircraft at a time in the hope they would not catch all of us. Some were to go low-level, some high. I was in the second wave and went for high. By the time I had climbed past the 7000 feet (outside the funnels and which with only 145HP took quite a time), the first wave was well gone. You could hear the chatter on the radio as the Slingsbys dived on them and read out their callsigns.

Nose down and I was just under 7000 feet as I went through the first funnel. VNE of the Cessna is 151 knots and I was soon approaching that, but by then the Slingsbys had dissipated their energy by chasing the first wave. They were the 67B models and although aerobatic, only 118HP, so once they had dived to catch their prey, they had spent their energy, and they could not climb quick enough to reposition.

I whistled over them hoping they would not look up and if they did, could not read my underwing registration. The radio stayed quiet, and I was through the second funnel in double-quick time. Later, Gerry Mulligan, the officer in charge, handed out some fine certificates.

Next day was an early departure for Midden Zeeland to lunch, then Earls Colne and Wellesbourne. Maybe the RAF had not wanted me previously, but now I had beaten them.

Two months later I had hooked up with the Avon Flying School (which later became Take Flight). They had a convenient clubhouse right next to where I parked the

Cessna and I discovered they also liked jollies – the first one we would share would be to the Kilkenny Rally. I already loved flying in Ireland, and the people there, and Avon were a fun crowd.

Routing via Cardiff, Kilkenny was 3.5 hours away. By the time we got there and checked into the Kilkenny Hotel it was time for the evening entertainment. The evening was hosted by the local Smithwick's Brewery – all the alcohol was free, and it would start at 7 o'clock sharp and dinner would be at 9 o'clock soft – this meant about 10.30. The local beer was delicious (the brewery had been bought by Guinness in 1965) and very few held back.

Which was a pity, as the navigation competition was next morning. There was no rush to start, and it was nearly three in the afternoon before I had a go, coming third. It would be two years later that I returned and managed second. Maybe Ireland was just too green for me to recognise targets.

Sunday was via Waterford for duty-free fuel and Cardiff for clearance. Twelve days later and it was Granite City again.

Another month and it was back to Ireland for the Galway Fly-in via Cardiff again. Part of the festivities here was a "tight squeak" competition. The idea is that you place two poles (on stands) on the taxiway at the narrowest distance that you think you can taxi through, which you then attempt. Touch a pole with a wingtip and you are out. As you pass between the poles you stop, and the judges measure each distance from tip to pole and the winner has the smallest clearance total.

This seemed too easy, as if you know your aircraft is 36 feet 2 inches wide, it is relatively simple to pace out the difference between the poles and I was surprised at how many people touched them. Maybe it would be tougher if you had to remain in the cockpit and direct others to position the poles, but we were in Eire.

Galway was always a bit quirky. On a later visit I won a pair of crystal glasses – one my RT and one for the best-looking co-pilot.

You've got to be joking, CAA?

As 1992 arrived I was approaching the important number of 700 hours flown. The old system for gaining a commercial licence by the improver route still existed. Rather than go for an official commercial course, you could become a commercial pilot by taking the exams and flight test and could immediately start earning money for flying. If you took the full set of exams for ATPL, you could become a frozen ATPL until you had 1500 hours, being paid for whatever commercial stuff you did whilst building hours.

The RAF may not have wanted me, but surely the airlines would? First step was to make sure I would be able to achieve a Class 1 medical, and for this you had to go to the CAA Medical Division at Gatwick, with associated costs.

Dr Hughes was most helpful, and after many hours of tests, I was told that I was definitely fit, but could not have a medical certificate and indeed my Class 2 might need to be withdrawn. The problem was a restriction in movement of my right shoulder. This has been shattered in the accident and was bolted together successfully, but it no longer had the ideal ball and socket arrangement that allowed full movement so I could raise my arm fully above my head (I could reach perhaps a foot higher with my left arm).

I was incredulous that this should be a stopper, as I had been flying for years with it like that, and it had never been a worry. They wanted to discuss the matter and thought that I might be able to fly again if I had a medical flight test on every type I flew, and they would let me know. It was a good job they had not done the blood pressure test after they told me.

Returning home, I had to keep badgering them for a decision, and they conceded that as I had been flying the Cessna for eight years without problem, they would allow me to continue, for now.

Eventually, I got the decision I needed from Dr Janvrin. The letter stated that they thought I should be able to fly any single engine aircraft without difficulty (although some Austers with a trim wheel in the roof might be difficult). And if I were flying commercially then I would be type rated on whatever I flew, and any difficulties would show up in that test.

Their remaining worry was if I took a group B rating on my PPL and flew twins. The point was there were several twins with complex overhead panels that I might not reach, and as PPL I would not need a flight test – so if I wanted to do the rating, I had to inform them, and they would need to work out how I could have individual flight tests for each type.

Enclosed with the letter was my Class 1 certificate. I shelled out for the Bournemouth ATPL correspondence course.

At the time, my day job was really suffering. We had had a year-long slump in the construction industry and commercial flying was to be a way out and although it might take a couple of years to get there, the idea of being paid to fly had great appeal. I had only just started into the volumes of learning supplied by Bournemouth when work picked up and all the time that I had had free suddenly disappeared. Making up for lost time (and money) I started rushing around the country again and studies went on the back burner.

By the time I got round to it again, the airline business was going through one of its slack periods, and when I looked at opportunities, just about the only people hiring were Air UK who had right-hand seats in Fokker Friendships to be had – but at way less than I was earning now work had picked up. I know you need to start somewhere, and need to gain seniority to really earn, but this would not even pay the mortgage and I would have to pay for exams, flight test, IR etc. It was a no-brainer – I just had to keep earning enough to pay for my flying as I always had.

Check Six – Marchetti!

Fighter Pilots USA operated from Kissimmee. The instructors were all F-16 pilots and told me the Siai-Marchetti SF.260D was the closest thing (non-jet) to play with. The courses they ran included the one I experienced, ACM1 Air Combat Manoeuvres, and if your company booked a whole day or more, they would run a corporate Top Gun challenge. By the time I arrived, they had some 400 "graduates" of which 30% were non-pilots. The rest were mainly private pilots like me wanting to have some fun.

I checked in with Tim Des Marais, Chief Pilot, to confirm my booking, and was lucky enough to see the debrief session of John "Pappy" Teeft who had travelled from Michigan to be their oldest graduate at 75. Seeing the fun he had had heightened my anticipation of the planned flights three days later. I knew it would be on schedule because the Florida weather is so reliable. Needless to say, the night before my appointment with the bandit, America's "Storm of the Century" blew through, killing 45 people in Florida alone, and totalling light aircraft all across the state. A DC-3 even flipped onto its back and Richard Branson's Vintage Airways Dakota suffered control damage – I had been due to fly to Key West on this – guessed I would have to try on another visit.

We rescheduled for 0800 Sunday and the bitterly cold northwest wind meant we had serious visibility of probably 50 miles. My instructor Mark "Mo" Lester was pleased at the prospect of extra "lifties and thrusties" that the cooler air would give us. Must be an America technical term?

My opponent was going to be "Roy-Boy" from Tampa – he was christened "Roy-Boy" at the debrief because he was such a natural, like the Robert Redford character of the same name. That probably explains why I got blown away so easily in fight number two.

Mo gave us the initial brief lasting about an hour, covering basic terminology, manoeuvres, and rules. Very comprehensive, an hour is about enough, as the conceptual side gets difficult for us civilians. The main points learnt are that we are about to fight the "manly" fight – guns only – no smart weapons. Our objectives are simple: Kill the Bandit by 1) Keeping Tally-Ho, 2) Executing Game-plan, 3) Taking Valid Shots. More importantly we must survive by 1) Keeping Tally-Ho, 2) Neutralising Bandit, 3) Not Giving Up.

Keeping Tally-Ho (sight) of the bandit is everything. Lose sight – lose fight. High and low yo-yos are discussed. Performed correctly they will position me for a good skeet shot by putting Roy-Boy in my sights, by solving range and angle problems. We cover the rules of engagement, including what to do if a bogey (unidentified aircraft) enters the combat zone, and we are told that for safety we should imagine a 500-foot bubble around the airplanes. Supposedly closer than that is too close – but more of that later.

For the non-pilots there are simple instructions – virtually no rudder is necessary, so just put the stick where you want it to go. With it pointed correctly at your opponent, the lift vector will put you inside his circle and ready for the kill. The stall is hard to obtain and never mentioned. The non-pilot hears about the "tickle" – a slight tremble when he is getting the most out of the airplane. This is when "God is dropping pebbles on the wing". When he is dropping rocks, your airspeed is slowing, and the other guy will catch you. When the boulders fall you are about to be shot or fall out of the sky anyway!

The performance of the Marchetti is such that the only real problem is overcontrolling. She will loop from straight and level effortlessly.

Once we have our basic knowledge, Roy-Boy splits off with Iceman (Kim Heishman) and I huddle with Mo to talk game-plans. We are going to fight fair first time, but in the second fight, kid them into the turn, then go vertical. Sounds easy but then Mo has more than 3000 hours. We suit up, choose helmets, and go for the photo-opportunity. A quick brief on the parachute and how we are not going to need it and we are strapped in and ready to go.

I had explained to Tim that I really wanted to do as much of the flying as possible and he told that for insurance purposes they were supposed to do the take-off and landing. Funny thing is, when I watch the video, I could swear I was doing it. (When I flew with Eddie Hammond in his WACO a few years earlier he had a similar insurance problem. We were not allowed to do aerobatics, but if I found myself in an unusual attitude it was OK to recover….).

We go for the formation take-off, waggle wings at our better halves as we pass over base, and head for the combat zone. Enroute, we practice tail chases and yo-yos and fire off a few shots. With your opponent in the centre ring of the gun sight, you are at perfect range, squeeze the trigger, try to say "guns, guns, guns" calmly, and what do you know, his smoke comes on and he is dead. Roy-Boy and I have a few shots at each other before reaching the killing ground. Meanwhile our instructors are operating tiny video cameras, alternately filming through the gun sight and the in-cockpit view. The gun sight shots will be used at debrief to confirm our kills or otherwise.

All too soon we are ready to start. At 6000 feet we pass head on and call "Fight's On!", immediately turning for each other and trying to get the lift vector just right. Roy and I seem evenly matched, and we stay opposite sides of the circle. This becomes a Lufbery – a descending circle that no-one can win. Forget Tom Cruise "turn and burn" – that would only give your opponent an easy shot. The alternative is to change plane, so we straighten out and go vertical, Roy-Boy following. Follow my leader loops gradually creep lower and Mo calls out a warning about height. I roll into horizontal and pull out at 2200 feet. Roy-Boy pulls too hard, goes inverted and crashes through the 2000 foot hard-deck. Never shot him, but I still won.

Fight two we were going to go with the game-plan, but Roy-Boy cheats by turning before the fight was called and we go vertical. Roy follows and after several loops I start to lose it. All of a sudden, we are like a falling leaf and although I recover, my stomach starts to make me lose interest. I slow and get picked off. About now I need the canopy open for fresh air. We take some time while I ready myself for the final encounter. I have never been airsick in my life and do not intend to start now – how come I feel so bad? Tim later explains that it is probably the "control thing" that most pilots have – a need to be in charge of events – and things up here were happening too fast for my liking.

I get my head straight and we are ready for number three. I am not going to last much longer so it is time to really cheat. Mo shouts to start the turn before we are even level and several yo-yos later, he's filling my sights for a snap shot, the pipper sounds, and yee-hah – Roy-Boy is dead! This was easier but I still need the canopy back to cool down while I loosen the chinstrap, and flight suit, to try and get comfortable.

It is almost bingo fuel (just enough to get home) so we practice close formation on the way back. Barrel-rolling over each other makes for great video shots on the in-cockpit camera, and we give each other a battle-damage inspection. I have not hurled my cookies yet and am starting to feel better.

Back at Kissimmee we do a formation flyby and break to land. At last, something I can cope with more easily, a curving fighter approach and the nose-up flare is similar to my 172, just nearer the ground and quicker. I cannot get this wrong and with Mo's coaching manage to land on the right side of 33 so Roy and Iceman can use the left. Formation taxi back to ops where our wives are waiting. As we swing round to park and they are in front of us, Mo says "here's an opportunity to shoot your wife". I have regretted immediately saying "guns, guns, guns" ever since Jean watched the video.

The debrief was probably as much fun as what went before. And the chair was more stable. Both pilots' videos are synchronised and shown simultaneously on side-by-side televisions. With full sound from both cockpits, you can see the whole relevance of what you were trying to do to each other, how the other guy cheated, and most importantly, did you really go down in flames? The pained expressions in high G are a delight to behold.

At the conclusion you are given not just the video, but a certificate of completion endorsed with your squadron "name". The name is given by your fellow pilots and instructors, should be sufficiently demeaning and reflects your flying characteristics. In USA there is a toothpaste called Close-up and as my aggression meant I got up close too often, with an in-your-face attitude – I became "Colgate".

It had been the best $600 I had ever spent, but I still wanted that Spitfire flight.

A Tiny Bit More Florida

Kissimmee has even more possibilities than Fighter Pilots USA. Jack Kehoe has a great Harvard (or SNJ-5 to be exact, being the Navy version) you can rent, and which was *the* trainer before flying Mustangs. Elsewhere, I have mentioned the WACO at KISM. And of course, Stallion 51 and the Warbird Museum are there.

Space Center (that is their spelling) was where I flew the PA-44 Cougar.

If you want to fly different types, Florida is the place. Cheap packages abound and the family can be entertained in theme parks whilst you make your own adventures. Anyone who ever wants to fly seaplanes will go to Jack Browns at Gilbert Field/Winter Haven – it is almost compulsory – but if it makes you fall in love with Piper Cubs there are wheeled versions available.

From Naples I rented with an instructor, and we flew the lakes. With the windows folded up and the doors down, we could hang our legs out in the warm sunshine. John knew just where yachts would be by the trees at the edge of the lakes, with their owners sunbathing nude on deck. He thought it was funny to glide down over the trees until over the boat and then put on full power – resulting in a rapid scramble to cover up with towels. We were not being voyeurs as we were too high to see anything except the panic!

Goodwood and the CAA (again)

The regular rallyists kept in touch if they knew of anything special happening, and one such occasion was a surprise party for Jim King's wife, Margaret. She was turning fifty and that coincided with Goodwood putting on an Aviator's Dinner Dance. Lots of us booked tickets for the dance and accommodation at the stately home/hotel nearby and flew into the airfield on the day.

Margaret was duly surprised to see us all at the venue and we had a great night. But the following morning the visibility was rubbish. Des Russell, from Fenland had appointments to keep and insisted on leaving. He taxied out in his Mooney to the chagrin of the Goodwood instructors and staff. At one point they radioed him to stop, claiming they had witnessed a prop strike, but it was just a ploy to try to convince him not to go.

The ploy did not work, and he took off and was in clear air as soon as he reached 500 feet or so and made his appointment on time. Immediately after he departed the instructors all started pouring through their Air Law books to see what offence he had committed and then reported him to the CAA. The rest of our group simply waited for the fog (did I say fog – I meant mist) to clear, and then went home.

Next thing was that we were all contacted as "witnesses to the offence" and were to be interviewed. A CAA investigator (an ex-policeman) came to my office by appointment, and I had my logbook with me as demanded, which he examined to ensure that I had no faults he could criticise and there were no notes about the visibility on that day. He complimented me on the neatness of my records…….

As Des was not a commercial pilot the offence was that he had taken off in visibility of less than 1500m and I was asked to make a statement of what the visibility had been. I could not, as I had no way of measuring it. "Do you think it was less than 1500m?" "It was certainly a little misty, but I wasn't on the runway, as no-one else was, so only Des could assess what he could see". Mr CAA accepted my position, and the interview was over.

Des was also interviewed of course and was questioned as to whether he understood the safety aspects, of not being able to see anything. He pointed out that neither could he see anything at night when flying over the fens, and when asked what he would have done had the propellor stopped, he replied that he would blow some of his cigar smoke into it to remedy the situation. Typical Des.

He was subsequently fined £500 due to the Goodwood staff testimony, and advised that if appointments could be that urgent, maybe he should consider buying a helicopter. He did just that, selling Mooney G-JAKI to David Abrahamson in Dublin, who has since sold it to Germany.

G-JAKI had been registered after he met Jacquie at one of the rallies and fell in love, married her, and bought the Mooney. Some years later, Jacquie succumbed to cancer, and Des decided he could not live without her. Another one lost.

Barry Davies and Trim

Amongst my new pilot friends at Wellesbourne was Barry, who enjoyed fine food and partying and invited Jean and myself to an excellent restaurant near him where he was well-known as a weekly visitor. Having discovered he also liked Guinness, I suggested we should enjoy some where it tastes best – Ireland.

Trim is a lovely grass strip of 540 metres just outside the Dublin ATZ and they were having a fly-in a few weeks later. We planned to route via Liverpool to clear customs and special branch and then land at Dublin before hopping over to Trim.

We were not very far from Wellesbourne when we found a squall-line stretched across our route. We could hear the lightning in our headsets and see the flashes. It looked like an early return, but there was a gap and despite having read of "sucker holes" we gave it a try. On the other side it was perfect calm and bright, and we touched down in Liverpool after an hour's flight.

Since the Aberdeen/Cranfield/Pooley incident I had always been keen on making sure about weather, and when we looked at the latest forecast for our destination it was not promising. So much so that we called Dublin ATC to check if our IMC rating would suffice. They simply told us we would have to file IFR if we wanted to come. Debate about IMC ratings meant nothing – just file IFR they said. We duly filed with flight rules "Z" – VFR to start, becoming IFR at Liffy as we would enter Shannon FIR.

It was mid-June 1993 and a balmy evening in Liverpool as we started to taxi. As we did our power checks at the threshold, suddenly the visibility dropped considerably. Tower called us, gave us the bad news that we already knew, and asked our intentions. Our Special VFR request was accepted, and we launched. Very quickly we were above the lower layer and below a higher one and the weather was still bright and smooth. We never even saw the Isle of Man, but it was pleasant flying. Until we got to Liffy.

As we crossed into Irish airspace the rain began to teem down and the skies blackened. With less than 30 miles to run we reported our border crossing and requested entry and an ILS. It was granted but within a few seconds of us attaining the glide slope a voice with a wonderful Irish brogue asked "Delta India – can you keep your speed up, I've a 737 up your arse?" we really did not want to have to go around so complied as best we could. We broke out at 800 feet to see the lights, and the brogue voice said, "Beware deep water on the runway".

I had never heard something sound as serious as that, and sure enough as we touched down and I concentrated on not aquaplaning, Barry told me he could see bow-waves coming off the wheels. We had just exited the runway as the 737 splashed down. We needed to follow the taxiway lights to parking it was so dark. And with rainfall like a tropical monsoon, we sat in the aeroplane and waited.

It did not stop and eventually we decided to get thoroughly soaked and get to the terminal. Once inside we could not believe how many people were there – it was wall to wall with people.

We soon learned that the road to the airport had been washed out. Any passengers that had flown in, could not leave. Lots of passengers who had arrived early hoping to go somewhere, could not – because their flight crews had no way to get to the airport. We later learnt that the weather had been so atrocious, that in Dublin town a toddler had been washed down a culvert and sadly drowned. The 737 behind us was the last plane to land that day and the airport was then closed to traffic. We had picked our day, hadn't we?

What do several thousand Irish people do when they cannot go anywhere? Go to the bar, of course! The queues to be served were enormous, and it was obvious that we would be waiting until morning to get to Trim, so approached the only hotel inside the airport - who unsurprisingly told us they were fully booked. After returning to the desk several times, we managed to persuade them that anyone who had not arrived was now unable to, and by two in the morning they gave us a room, but only a double. Barry and I tossed a coin to see who would be under the sheets and who on top.

Next morning the weather was better, but not much. We needed to get to Trim and kept asking ATC to let us out. Eventually they gave in as long as we filed IFR again. We would never actually need any height, as Trim was just 20 miles away. All we needed to do was to hop over the hedge.

As we lined up, we were cleared "IFR departure not above 3000 feet" and duly cleared said hedge. From brakes off to brakes on was just 20 minutes, but I did manage to log five minutes instrument flying.

The people at Trim were amazingly welcoming and seemed really grateful that we made it as they had put a lot of effort into the organisation, and a ceili with bands and dancing had been arranged for Saturday night. The Guinness that night was welcome, superb, and we never paid for one – our generous hosts made sure of that.

It had been a remarkable arrival, but the following morning we discovered we were not the only visitors. Somehow three aircraft from Sleap had flown directly into Trim, avoiding all the clearances they were supposed to do, and navigating though the atrocious weather using

some new-fangled equipment called GPS. I was going to
have to get one of those.

Stornoway

Always on the look-out for opportunities to offset costs, in late October I was pleased to get a call about a decorator problem that needed visiting. I had never imagined that people did anything to a lighthouse, other than paint it, but this one was having wallpaper problems, and it was on the Isle of Lewis.

The decorator had left site, so it was not immediately urgent, and it was agreed I could visit at the weekend. It would be a long flight to make alone, so after enquiring in our clubhouse if anyone were interested, suddenly the aircraft would be full. We would have to stay over Saturday night and return next day, so booked a suitable guest house. I also had to clear it with the Highlands and Islands Authority to be allowed to land at all, but importantly, to be allowed to take off on the Sunday when the airfield is closed.

All set with a 7 a.m. start, it was Wellesbourne to Cumbernauld for fuel and then on to Stornoway, with breathtaking scenery of mountains and lochs en route. Four and a half flying hours of sheer pleasure, and we were on the island by 12.30. The purpose of the visit took less than a couple of hours as it was obvious how the decorator had messed up. I demonstrated the correct method, and he was satisfied and accepted blame.

Stornaway is about the only populated area of the island, and as the guest house was close by, we went into town for Saturday night. It was like Newcastle! Throngs of youngsters (and older) filled the streets clutching pints. Cars cruised up and down the High Street stopping when they saw talent. It was a modern Sodom and Gomorrah.

Next morning there was not a soul to be seen. We enquired of our landlady if she could call us a cab to go to the airport. "There's no transport on a Sunday – it's the

Lords Day. And there's no flights either – you can't go anywhere except church". We gently explained that we had our own aircraft and permission to leave on a Sunday but needed to get to the airport. Her eyes lit up. "I've always wanted to fly in a wee aircraft!".

The deal was done. She drove us to the airport. I took her for a fifteen-minute tour above Lewis and as she waved us off, we departed for Cumbernauld again. The excitement was not quite over as to clear the mountains I had to get above a layer of cloud, and as we neared Cumbernauld there were no breaks. Using the VOR at Glasgow we descended over Loch Lomond where I knew the high ground was either side and the loch was wide. Only just in time as when we started down Jack Frost was making his appearance on the windscreen. Five minutes of IMC and we were in the clear and perfectly over the centre of the loch.

Time for a Change?

I was coming up for 900 hours, the majority in my 172. It was the time that Eastern Bloc aircraft started being bought and brought to the west. At Wellesbourne there was a Yak-52 being demonstrated by a Russian aerobatic champion hoping to make some sales, so I invested in a 30-minute trial. Impressed, I told Jean I wanted one.

We were still debating a few weeks later when the new owner of the same aircraft I flew (RA-01337) aerobated it into the ground next to his home. The enquiry found he had removed some of the stops on the control surfaces to increase manoeuvrability – a fatal mistake, literally. Jean did not believe I should have one.

Nine months later, I had read about the Yak-18T. Now this sounded more likely. It was a four-seater but could still do aerobatics if I felt the need. I attended a Yak fly-in, and a kind gentleman allowed me 20 minutes hands-on in his Lithuanian 18T. It was pretty good, and he'd bought it very cheaply, but it was old.

Alan Cassidy at White Waltham was doing demonstration flights in a much newer one and I went for a trial in RA-44481. This was considerably better and was a smart black and gold machine. We rolled and looped, and Alan demonstrated his prowess. This was going to mean another discussion with Jean.

Only a couple of weeks into the debate, there was an air show at White Waltham. The same aircraft was doing a circuit, inverted, when it ran out of fuel. The pilot just had chance to roll right side up before it hit the ground and tore the wings off. I was keeping the Cessna.

Nordic Precision Championship

I had been slowly improving my Precision Flying. And the discipline constantly improved my results in less exacting competitions, but now we had an invite to go to Denmark. This was to be one of my longest flights, but I would share the route with Barry Davies (of Trim fame) and Adrian Ryman, who later became an ATCO at Essex Radar.

Outbound was via Norwich, then Groningen to reach Herning where the competition was to take place. It was almost six hours to get there and six to come back and most was over water. Whilst there, there were three precision courses and two sessions of landings. Another 4 hours flying. Sixteen hours in four days and Delta India was working hard. Her fifty-hour check was due whilst we were there, so we used the 10% extension to gain another five hours and scraped back to Wellesbourne with ten minutes to spare.

The competition was extremely well run. They take it very seriously in that part of the world and because it was the Nordic Championship, although we were allowed to score, we were not part of the championship itself. Hospitality was marvellous and I managed to beat the Finns at least.

But the most exciting part of the competition happened during the landings. We were all spaced out at ten metres apart either side of the landing box, to do the judging. An enthusiastic Danish Maule pilot landed OY-CTT very hard, rolled out of the box, put the power on and went round for his next attempt. The damage must have been done on the first, because as he touched down on the next, there was a loud crack and his port undercarriage folded up completely, his wing hit the ground, and the aircraft slewed round heading directly at the judges. We scattered.

The pilot seemed non-plussed. He got out, cursing his engineer. "I told him to change those bolts!" Apparently, the Maule has retaining bolts that hold the undercarriage in place that need changing every 100 hours or so as they can fail (or quicker if you make hard landings!).

The top surface of the port wing was wrinkled as the aircraft was resting on the tip, but despite that, new bolts were found, volunteers lifted the wing, and the bolts were inserted so it stood square again.

The wing looked remarkably straight, and being a taildragger, the prop had not grounded, so he started up and tried again.

Next time he landed out of the box, but very gently.

Metalwork

A year after inserting the AO nails into my femurs following my bathroom drama, the hospital requested I visit again to have them removed, but with previous experience in mind, I had refused. But now I was getting a little problem. My right hip had always rubbed a bit and it was getting worse. It seemed the nail was protruding a little from the head of the femur (maybe they had not hammered it in hard enough?) and that was causing the irritation in the socket of my hip.

It only took two days recovery after they pulled them out through my buttocks. A couple of stitches where they had opened me up to insert the threaded tool and simply pull the tubes out. Sterilised in the autoclave, the nails were given to me as a souvenir. Because the right-hand nail had been rubbing and under pressure, a stress fracture had commenced several inches down from the top. A hollow tube, the crack had already spread around 70% of the circumference. If I had not had it removed when I did, there was a chance they would never have been able to remove the bottom section.

Nobody at Wellesbourne knew of my accident nor that I had just been in hospital. I took my "trophies" into the clubhouse, placed them on the bar, and sat down awaiting people's curiosity. One by one, the members had a look and I queried whether they could find the fault. Yes, they could see the crack but had no idea what they were looking at "Have you been flying with this?" "Crikey, that could have gone at any minute". I left them to work out which part of the aircraft had been about to fail, then our CFI appeared, found the flaw and admitted he had no idea what the parts were "Something to do with the rudder?" he asked.

I confirmed they did assist in steering with the rudder pedals then came clean, to everyone's amazement that these lumps of metal had come out of me.

Our CFI (let's call him John) became a commercial pilot and years later was rostered with another buddy of mine (let's call him Dave) who I knew from Earls Colne. The pair were to take a shed (Shorts 360 aircraft) on a freight run from Stansted to Dusseldorf in the middle of the night, delivering newspapers and picking up a small quantity of Ford motor parts. I jumped at the invitation to join them and once we were airborne, John decided to go in the back for a sleep and suggested Dave let me have a go at flying the Sherpa.

It was the first time I had used an HSI, and Dave persuaded me to slow one of the engines to see the effect and how I would need to control asymmetry. Bear in mind, I was not twin rated and had no experience of turbine engines, so it was a good job Dave was alert when I managed to shut one engine down completely.

Despite my faux pas, newspapers were delivered, and 5 kilos of parts returned to Stansted. The impression I was left with, was that had I ever managed to go commercial, being a freight jockey would be much more fun and preferable to being a bus driver.

Piper vs Cessna

I am not exactly a "pot-hunter", but I do like competitions. Once I had relocated to Wellesbourne, I began organising teams from there, to enter Jersey and Guernsey Rallies with some success. One of my previous team members asked if I would navigate for him in a forthcoming competition for Piper owners. The new Piper distributor at Bournemouth, Anglo American Airmotive were about to run a day and had invited Piper owners from across the country.

Much as I would have liked to help, I am not a very good passenger. In truth, I am scared of heights, tall buildings, and a cable car is my nemesis. But when I am in control, I am totally fine (the trouble with a cable car is if that rope snaps, what can I do? But if my engine quits, I know how to glide). Before I gently said no, I contacted Anglo American to see if their competition day was exclusively for Pipers and explained I had a Cessna.

Seems I was an ideal target customer, and I should come and see their wonderful machines, and so it was that Jean and I arrived at Hurn in July. There were five aspects to the competition, and each was a fiver to enter – this was to go to charity and the prizes were provided by the distributor. With £25 invested I was up against 54 Pipers and one other Cessna. The worry about the Cessna was that it was to be flown by Malcolm Evans, an experienced BPPA pilot from Haverfordwest. He had obviously asked the same question as I did and been accepted.

I cannot remember all the competitions, but they included a timed circuit, and one was a raffle, but I did come third in the spot landing and the prize was £25. I had my money back! What I had really come for was the Navex. It was a long day with so many competitors in turn and we did not get airborne until around three o'clock. An hour later we were back and one of the last, so just waited for the results.

The awards were made and when it came to the last prize which was for the Navex, they called me up to receive the Piper Cup (but did not mention my registration nor aircraft type as they had for all the others). The young lady Jean had been chatting to, knew something we did not, and began to congratulate her on our good fortune and how wouldn't we have a great time in Florida?

Sure enough, alongside the beribboned trophy there was a certificate that declared "You have won a holiday in Florida for Two Persons and a tour of The Piper Aircraft Factory. Up to a maximum of $1,500. To claim your prize contact etc." Well, blow me down with a feather.

I will come back to the subsequent visit, but the Piper Cup story was not over. A year later, being on the list of previous entrants, I received an invitation to try again – but amongst the points mentioned was "only for Piper aircraft". They had also changed the prizes, as someone had pointed out that the highest allowable prize for sporting aviation was £500. I had been more than lucky the previous year.

They still allocated the same overall value, but it was £500 for the winner, £300 second and the runner-up was to get £200. None of those were to be sniffed at, so I found a Wellesbourne school prepared to rent me their PA28-161 (G-BTNE) provided I passed a check ride. Three days after I demonstrated that I could fly something other than a Cessna I was in Bournemouth again. It all went rather well and the second Piper Cup and £500 were mine!

Then came the rub. With check-out, transit both ways, and competition I had amassed nearly five hours on the rental and the bill was £490. Maybe only a tiny profit, but a lot of free flying and fun had been had.

The Piper Factory Visit

Using my British Airways Amex card on everything I spent had gained me many BA Miles. We were allowed to use the $1500 prize in any way we wanted, so with a combination of airmiles and cash we had enough to take Jean's widowed mum with us. Rose was a lovely, funny northern lady, just five foot nothing, and when we turned left on the Boeing 747 she was almost swallowed by the Club Class seat. A steward took a shine to her, kept her well topped up with champagne throughout the flight and even gave us a bottle to slip into our bag before we got off.

Orlando was the only place to stay. We knew our way around and there was always something interesting to hire. Rose stayed at the hotel whilst Jean and I drove to Vero Beach and Piper. In my youth I use to visit the production line for Hawker Siddeley 125s at Chester (Hawarden) which was much bigger, but the Piper line was fascinating. There were not that many new fuselages being manufactured (they were just coming out of Chapter 11), but you could sense the passion they had for the product, and a brand-new aircraft is just so nice.

Heritage was important to them too, and they had just totally restored the original Piper Cub. It made my Cessna look weary.

Part of the day was supposed to be lunch with Chuck Suma, their President. We chatted to him, and there was a slight embarrassment when he asked us which Piper we had won the competition in. He was also busy with lawyers, to do with them bringing the company out of Chapter 11, so asked to be excused lunch. We were taken to the nearby golf club for lunch by his sales director, and as an apology were allowed free rein of the Pilot Shop. "Help yourself to anything you want". "Anything?"

Shirts, caps, keyrings, stickers, books – all came home with us.

We did not get chance to fly anything at Vero Beach, so once back at Orlando I spoke to a school at Orlando Executive that had a very nice (and familiar) 172 – N212FS. I wanted to go to the Florida Keys where Ernest Hemingway used to live and was happy to take an instructor with me for local knowledge and save all the certification, providing I could do all the flying, which I did.

When I asked if they had anyone to accompany me to the Keys, there was no shortage of volunteers, and a lad probably half my age, and newly qualified as an instructor, explained he had never been there and would love to go. The deal was struck, and we set off down the east coast, with a stop at Palm Beach County (and a touch and go at Valkaria). After three and half hours flying, we were at Key West and soon to be in the famous Sloppy Joe's.

With a tick in that box, we set off up the west coast for Venice, with a touch and go at the Everglades en route. Then it was Kissimmee but by then it was dark before I landed, so we decided I should revalidate my night rating.

After ten minutes on the ground, I did three touch and goes and then back to Orlando Executive for another touch and go then a full stop. An excellent seven and half hours in the air but boy, was I in trouble when I got back to the hotel. It had been dark for a very long time and the girls had no idea where I was.

The rest of our time in Orlando was mainly enjoying the delights of Church Street Station. This was an area of town (now gone) dedicated to themed entertainment such as the Cheyenne Saloon, where you could enjoy drinking your Flaming Hurricane whilst watching the line-dancing.

There was an aviation theme too, and their aircraft were constantly overhead skywriting "Church St" and the like. In their hangar was the most beautiful Beech Staggerwing I have ever seen.

Rose had the time of her life, but on a couple of occasions she did not feel well, and we thought the sickness was caused by all the travel. Some months after we brought her back home, she passed away with stomach cancer. She had never complained about the pain nor given any clues, and I am just so grateful that my passion for flying had allowed us to give her a good time.

Disagreements at Work

I was now a director of the company that I had originally partnered with. The owner had continued to earn fabulous profits from our efforts and was soon a multi-millionaire. His love was sailing, and he had bought an ocean-going yacht that he kept in Portugal. Now he wanted to spend his time with it, so promoted me to managing director, and his time was free. He still owned everything and was really in charge, but mine was the desk that complaints would reach.

The first few years went reasonably well, but then came another massive slump in the construction industry and our turnover dropped by more than a third. I was accused of getting it wrong, but there just was not business to be had. At least not in UK. But there was a boom in the Middle East and we agreed that I should visit Dubai to find new business and distributors, which I did and restored our fortunes (well, his fortune to be exact).

But I was never forgiven, because he had to come back into the MD role whilst I travelled and had to forsake his yacht. I achieved an amazing stock order from a distributor based in Dubai (mainly UK ex-pats who also had a Thai partner). It was the biggest order we had ever had, and for a short time I was a hero. Then we did not get paid on time. The distributor claimed cashflow problems. I knew it was not a problem and that we would eventually be paid, as if you renege on a debt in Dubai, you are jailed until you pay up. Eventually the cash was paid, but I had been subject to daily browbeating about the situation, and I knew I would have to move to pastures new.

When I had been made a director, I had been awarded convertible shares, provided I signed an agreement not to work for competition in the UK. The owner was a litigious sort, and no doubt would try to use this if I left, so it was fortunate that I heard of a role for a wallcovering manufacturer who needed an export salesman – the work would be outside the UK.

I really enjoyed resigning and explaining that he could not touch me! But it did mean relocation, from Warwickshire to Kent to be near the factory, and Delta India's new home became Rochester Airport in 1997.

Keeping the Customer Satisfied

One of my major customers had been Hilton Hotels. Miss Turner was responsible for selecting interior design products for their purchasing department and we had chatted about visiting one of the factories where we produced their wallcovering. But I was now going to work directly for a manufacturer and wanted to ensure Hilton would remain my customer.

We arranged the trip as my last function in the week I was leaving the old firm. I was to fly her into Welshpool which was only a mile from the factory. Sandie Johnson was the factory boss, and did not even know there was an airport, and then realised it was "Bob Jones's field". By the time we got there to be collected by him, he had been tipped off that I had just resigned, so although pleased to see me he would only be able to show Miss Turner around the factory, as there were new products and processes that he did not want me to see.

I waited in reception whilst the tour was given, and when they emerged from the factory Sandie offered to take us both to the pub for some lunch. "What a shame! I have already arranged that we would fly round Snowdon and land at Carnaerfon for lunch. It's all booked".

"I cannae beat that" said Sandie in his broad Scottish accent. And so it was that within weeks, my first customer for the new company was Hilton. Aviation rules – OK?

I Like a Good Breakfast

Before I had left Wellesbourne, in between the formal competitions we scanned the magazines for events happening anywhere, whether fly-ins, spot-landings or whatever, and soon we discovered breakfast patrols. These popped up quite regularly and were at places like Sturgate, Thruxton and at Leicester it would usually be a brunch patrol. Other regulars were Seething and Elmsett. The deal was similar to the Laarbruch task, but you simply had to get into the circuit and announce your arrival, without being spotted, to earn your free breakfast (or brunch).

Our crews would set out en masse, and probably outnumbered the defendants on most occasions, so they did not know who to chase. We would have a plan to arrive at high level with radio silence, of course, and swoop in at speed. The Sturgate Yak was probably the hardest to beat but coming out of the sun at VNE usually led to a great fry-up.

These events seemed to peter out after a while, and I hope they will re-emerge as they are great social occasions. But there was one breakfast patrol scheduled to be at Leicester after I had moved to Rochester, and I thought I would make a solo effort. The forecast was not good with a front moving across the country, but my poorly educated guess was that by the time I reached Leicester it would have moved through and the event could happen. It would then clear across the country so I could get home.

Making full use of my IMC, I went northwest. I was between cloud layers most of the time and just occasionally could see the ground. The only airfield I saw en route was my old base at Little Staughton which appeared in a hole. With hindsight, I should have landed, but I had breakfast in my sights.

Forecasts are just that, and as I approached Leicester and nonchalantly called them for their weather (as a passing aircraft of course, not to give them a clue as to my arrival) the reply was fog. I did try a descent of sorts, but there was not a hole to be found and there was no choice but to turn round. I would land at Little Staughton, have a pee, and wait for the weather to clear.

Except that Little Staughton could no longer be seen. Oops. Cambridge was relatively close, and they could give me an SRA. They were happy to talk to me, but the SRA was impossible due to their radar being unserviceable. Double oops. The VOLMET frequency confirmed I'd really got it wrong – the front had stalled and everywhere was tricky. It had to be Southend, then. Trouble was that I was now getting desperate for facilities. The only thing I had available was a tray of desiccant that I kept in the aircraft to keep the avionics free from moisture.

With a lot of careful manoeuvring, I managed to fill the tray to the top, but it was really, really full. It was obvious that on landing it would spill so it needed to be emptied. Never, ever, ever try to empty anything out of the window of a moving aircraft – most of it simply blows back in and covers some of you and the back seat! But I was happier being wet (and probably smelly) than in pain, so in due course I took an SRA into Southend and landed safely.

The Strasser Scheme for free landings due to weather diversion was handy, and I waited outside for the weather to clear (so as not to offend staff with any smell), and eventually it did, and I could return to Rochester. But it had taken a long time and whilst my landing was free, the parking charge was quite hefty. On reflection, I could have bought a very good breakfast with that.

Pastures New

Rochester Airport had been the first place for an overnight once I had my licence. What was the Crest Hotel at the airport entrance had now become a Holiday Inn. We managed to find a village home some 20/25 minutes away. And then it was much of the same touring and competitions except that now my place of work could be abroad. This was a matter of mainly short trips into Europe to start with, which did not affect my flying, but gradually my area expanded, and I ended up with the world.

Before I had been at the new company very long, it was taken over by an American company and they wanted to impress some of us with a tour of their USA factories, which were all over the States. At the time they had their own airfield in Columbus Mississippi (GTR – General Tire Regional) and three company aircraft. We zipped around the country in N2G - a Hawker Siddeley 125 XT-700. This was a very quick version of the DH125s I had watched being built at Hawarden many years before. The company "van" collected you from the hotel, took you straight to the aircraft (with engines already running), and you were airborne in minutes. It certainly beat flying by airlines, and boy, did it climb!

Following the week in USA, my new role was decided – first Japan as well as Europe, and then once settled in, the rest of Asia and Africa. Australasia soon followed. The Americas would come later (as the new owners did not want UK product being sold into their own back yard).

This was going to be time-consuming, and if I was not to fly as much in UK, I would make sure that wherever I visited, I would try to fly something there. The first such was at Pretoria, South Africa – a familiar 172 (ZS-LZH) from Wonderboom Airport. New Zealand was another 172 (ZK-DFI) at Ardmore and Australia was a PA28

(VH-IJR) at Jandakot. The latter flight was only local, so two days later it was another 172 (VH-JZU) that took me to Busselton and Manjimup (there's a name to play with!). On the next visit it was Jabiru (VH-LSI) Avery to Camden and Hoxton Park. And so it went on, with the worst hire being HS-ATD a Cessna 150 at Bangphra, Thailand. It was a dog of a 150 and the strip had a mountain at one end and wires at the other. It would not accelerate on take-off, and I aborted. Once they had unjammed the brakes it was OK but not really a pleasure.

In between these flights I had to work, but I also took every opportunity to enjoy the flights there and back, amassing airmiles and trying just about every type of airliner. The A380 was remarkable. There were also joyrides to be had, such as the Beaver seaplanes at Sydney, where you flew down the river for lunch, or the helicopters out of Las Vegas where you went for breakfast in Grand Canyon. A dirty rotten job, but someone had to do it.

Concorde

Not long after we relocated it was our Silver Wedding anniversary. Jean had always tolerated my excessive amount of flying (and enjoyed a lot with me) and I wanted to make this special. I read about a company called Superlative Travel who specialised in Concorde charters. They did not ask for a lot of money but wanted people to enjoy the experience. They were organising a tour of Toronto which would end in a flight back on Concorde.

I approached Grant, my friendly travel agent (who booked my overseas flights etc) to see if he could help. He could. The outbound leg was to be by 747 to Toronto, of course. But I had by then accumulated untold numbers of BA miles, Star Alliance miles, and hotel points. We came up with a plan.

BA miles would take us to Boston in Club Class. We would stay for a couple of days at Swissotel where I had an upgrade certificate (they gave us a suite). We would be there for Independence Day and see the Proms in the Park and fireworks and follow the tourist trail to the scenes of the tea party. Then Star Alliance miles would take us to Toronto, where we would check into the Sheraton. This was part of the tour as organised by Superlative, but we would use the upgrade certificate I had for Sheraton (we got the club floor). Next morning, we would join up with the others on the tour.

Grant had negotiated a reduced price for me, as we would not need Superlative's seat to Toronto and even threw in his commission. Jean knew nothing of this, and I told her we were going on holiday but not where to. I had to tell her what to pack, but in due course we set off. At no stage during the week did I tell her what was next, and the first she knew where we were initially going, was when we got to Heathrow. Gradually each treat was revealed, but when we joined up with the other tour members, one of the first outings was a boat trip around Toronto Island. She struck up a conversation with the lady sat next to her, and would you believe it, she lived in Wellesbourne village!

"Exciting isn't it – going home on Concorde?" she said. Bugger, the surprise had gone. But there were some more – dinner atop the CN Tower, another in a revolving restaurant, underground shopping, then under Niagara Falls in a boat and over them in a Bell 407 helicopter, and the final night was the Phantom of the Opera. All in all, a cracking week, to be finished off in amazing style.

Toronto to Heathrow took 4 hours 15 minutes. Everyone aboard was there for the joy of it. We cheered as she went supersonic, then at Mach 2 and then when we reached 50,000 feet and could see the curvature of the earth. We all got to visit the cockpit, and were wined and dined superbly, before receiving a great deal of memorabilia. G-BOAD will be forever in our hearts.

Not bad for £900.

Undercarriage Trouble

One of the beauties of the 172 is that everything is "fixed and welded". No wobbly prop that needs servicing and no undercarriage that can fail to come down. But nothing is perfect, and when Clyde Cessna designed this one, he used flat spring steel for the undercarriage, but added a step to each side made of alloy. Being dissimilar metals, they corrode.

Usually not too badly – you might just see a rust line creeping through the paint – but you never know how bad it is underneath. That is until a heavy engineer, trying to top up the hydraulic fluid reservoirs behind the rudder pedals, pushes really hard against one and breaks it off. It was amazing just how much of the steel, the alloy step took with it. No doubt the starboard side would be just as bad underneath the paint, so they would both need replacing.

I am almost certain that the Cessna pricing policy for replacement parts is designed to stop the "heritage fleet" flying. Each leg would cost $4000 plus freight from USA and associated VAT & duty, plus installation of course. Just the U-bolt needed to secure (one each leg) is $450. It is unsurprising that there is a good trade in second-hand parts – but most are uncertified and whilst they might be nicely painted, who knows what lies beneath?

For many weeks whilst I trawled the web, whenever I flew, I landed ever so gently. Finally, I got lucky and found some USAF parts. A T-41 Mescalero (military 172) had just had a pair of brand-new legs fitted (with necessary documentation), and within weeks had been scrapped, for who knows why.

I needed to get the legs to the UK by the cheapest method and happened upon the eBay Global Shipping Programme. They collate bulk shipments of all sorts of goods and ship the whole lot economically to anywhere in the world, and take care of all paperwork, declarations etc and being used goods there is no duty to be paid. It is surprisingly efficient and quick.

Having arranged with the vendor to use them, I soon received two pristine legs, new steps and U-bolts – all for less than £500.

My engineer came good and agreed that he would paint them and fit them during the annual at very little charge. Woo-hoo!

A little Birthday Treat

Shortly after the following Guernsey Rally, we decided to extend and go further into France. We had pre-booked at Le Chateau La Chassagne, which we reached via Chartres. Le Chateau was a private strip with hotel alongside. The pilot owner of both strip and hotel would greet you on landing, load your luggage and you into a Rolls Royce and then drive around the corner (probably 100 yards) to the hotel.

Once checked in you had to meet on the steps of the hotel where you were to be inducted into the Confrerie Chateau la Chassagne. It was obligatory to wear a beret (supplied). Your job is to remove the cork from a champagne bottle – with an upward sweep of a cavalry sword – which you receive instruction about and is not that hard to do. You are rewarded with a medal on a red, white and blue ribbon, and your logbook receives a Checkpoint Charlie stamp.

A superb dinner was eaten later, and the breakfast was equally good. Just writing this prompted me to see if it still exists, but although the hotel may do, the airfield has been closed because of a new golf club. C'est la vie!

The return trip included a stop at Reims Prunay. We visited the fabulous cathedral, and it would have been rude not to take some produce from the home of champagne back with us. Reims was also where Delta India was built. We had taken her home for her thirtieth birthday.

Bentley Priory

It was shortly to be the 60th anniversary of the Battle of Britain and there was to be a charity auction of all sorts of memorabilia at RAF Bentley Priory. It was a grand affair, champagne reception included, and you had to buy tickets. But amongst the lots there were six half-hour flights in the Grace Spitfire, the dates to be arranged some time following payment.

It was also my fiftieth birthday and Jean made the decision. "Just go and spend whatever it takes". That is quite a lot of latitude. But I had a figure in mind that did not seem too excessive for the chance of a lifetime. Bear in mind there was nobody selling flights in military aircraft then.

The chap sat next to me had gone for the same reason. I seem to remember he flew from Cranfield. We chatted as we sat through the lots of paintings, medals, stamps, and everything else including jewellery. There were other flight opportunities available, but these were relatively ordinary such as a flight in a twin, or a helicopter trial lesson. We waited patiently for our main event.

When it eventually came round, I thought I should wait to see what the first one went for. We had agreed that if either of us won one – hopefully, both of us - the other would attend the flight to get some air-to-air photography of ourselves flying in the Spitfire. My seat companion won the first at £1500.

This was £500 more than I had thought of spending. But there were another five remaining. The bids rose each time with the final one going for £3500. I had been sat on my hands – it was far too rich for me.

We stayed in regular touch, and I would have kept my promise, but the flights never materialised. Insurance was the stopper – they would not risk it, so the buyers were offered refunds or if they were feeling generous and wished to forego it……

I had returned home thoroughly disappointed, but later reflected that it would have been even worse to have won the bidding, only to have the prize wrested away later.

Mud

Rochester is a fine airport but suffers from waterlogging, not only on runways but taxiways too. After really bad rains it can be closed for months. In January I had taken Delta India to Little Staughton for her annual. A month later and I still could not bring her home due to closure.

Manston had the biggest hard runway around and was not too many more miles from home. I made arrangements and relocated there for a time, which ended up as six months. I thought I would stay at Manston to solve the problem of being unable to fly whenever the weather gods decided, but it was not really the answer. It was soulless.

Although parked outside in the flying school area, you had to reach your aircraft through the school building. Which meant you were limited to flying when the school was open. At least there was a pool of people to enjoy flying with. Wrong. If you were not training or hiring aircraft, they did not want you there, and reception was frosty. Ted Girdler himself was a decent sort, but he sadly plunged into the sea in a Delphin at the Eastbourne Air Show.

Furthermore, whilst Manston's runway was enormously wide, it needed to be because the winds were nearly always across it. I had to find somewhere else.

That turned out to be Maypole, even closer to home – equidistant with Rochester but to the east of my village, rather than west like Rochester. Maypole was a grass strip of 500m and having a significant slope, drained well except for the bottom of the hill – but if you were not flying by then you were not going anywhere, anyway. It also had another 150m field at the top with a footpath across it, that you could use in summer when it was dry.

It was cheaper parking than Rochester and I no longer had a group to help with costs. I remained there for eight years despite the owners who were often difficult, and with whom you had to be careful. They regularly told people to leave when they were displeased with them, often for petty reasons. Despite that they had residents who remained for years, for the convenience of the location, but they are all gone now as the field was sold for development and the aircraft summarily evicted. Nice.

When the time was right for me, I moved back to Rochester Airport.

Isle of Man

There used to be an annual Air Rally held on the Isle of Man, but it was long before I got involved in such things. I had seen photographs which showed a trophy almost as tall as the winner. Then there was an announcement that in July 2002, they would be holding a rally, to coincide with an air race around the island.

I knew a few of the air racing fraternity but had only tried it once. I had raced against a few people from Gloucester, and they definitely cheated. Moreover, it seemed that the result really rested with the handicapper rather than the contestants. But the idea of a rally on the island had real appeal.

When Jean learned of the prize involved, she told me to book immediately. Always wishing to comply, I did and then received all the details. Rather than Ronaldsway, it was to be at Jurby the old airfield. The "rally" was really just a timed arrival, and that was to be challenging as a map with minute marks doesn't help much over the sea.

But since the Trim fly-in I had warmed to GPS and purchased a little Garmin 90 which would get me in the ballpark and with Jurby being at the northeast of the island, I could use a large-scale roadmap to plot the last few miles which would be overland, when minute marks would work. The task was to fly past the judges by the runway at the allocated time followed by a circuit and landing.

Liverpool took just over two hours, and then a little over an hour to the island. I thought I had made a pretty good fist of it and was even more certain when after parking and walking through the barriers I was greeted by Robert Millar, one of the Ultimate High pilots.

He demanded to know how well I thought I had done and said he was pretty sure he had been very close. Then he saw the BPPA sticker on my flight bag and groaned. "Oh God, do you know Rodney Blois?" Yes, I did, he was the Chairman (now sadly passed away). Robert was as keen to win as I was, and it was not until dinner we would know.

In due course, we had a feast, and the announcements were made. Robert had come a close second and won a flight in a Harvard. But I was just two seconds out, and received a cheque for £250, and was to report in the morning for my flight in the Spitfire!

At last. It was in the Welsh Spitfire IX PT462 (alias G-CTIX). Duly suited and helmeted we did loops, barrel rolls and half cuban above the island and I was allowed to handle. Just looking out at the elliptical wing as you pivoted around it was very emotional.

I had always wanted to compare with the Mustang, and I finally could. I would respectfully suggest that the Mustang was not just bigger, but smoother, slicker and a Cadillac of the sky, whereas the Spitfire was an E-type – harsh, raucous but completely iconic – and I was the luckiest so-and-so ever.

The following year they ran the competition again, but I was working that week. Robert won his Spitfire flight.

A Biblical Experience

Dubai was a regular hunting ground for work. I was there so regularly that I needed to ease the boredom and heard of a school at Fujairah that had a 172. It was across the mountains from Dubai, but that did not matter, we drove. Once there it was a quite new Cessna 172SP (A6-FAA), and I was surprised to learn it was running on Mogas in such a warm climate. There is no Avgas in the Emirates.

Again, I went with an instructor to save paperwork, and initially we flew a little into Omani airspace then back into the Emirates. On the west coast were the major airfields and we made touch and goes at all of them – Sharjah, Dubai, Abu Dhabi – all for absolutely no charge. Try landing at Heathrow for free (if at all!). Then we were heading back across the mountains.

There was something in front of us, that I have never seen before or since. Stretching from high altitude right down to the ground was what can only be described as a pillar of cloud. It must have been a couple of miles wide, but it had straight sides and rose vertically to the heavens. We could see lightning flashes inside it and where it met the ground there were eddies of sand being raised. It made me think of the pillar of cloud that led Moses out of the desert.

It was in between us and Fujairah and the instructor kept telling me to steer towards it. There was no way I would approach it and made a width berth, landing safely back at Fujairah.

There had been something of a language barrier, and I never got any explanation of what it was, or whether a regular occurrence. But on the drive home we saw some of the effects. It had rained, and at roundabouts there were four-wheel drives on their sides and roofs. Nowadays Dubai has its own micro-climate and rain is not unheard of, but back then these drivers just could not cope – they had driven at their usual breakneck speed and paid the penalty.

If any reader has any ideas about the "pillar of cloud", please let me know.

Alderney – Not by Choice

Whilst I was still based at Maypole, Jean and I attended another fun Guernsey Rally, but it was soon time for home on Sunday morning and we duly departed. As usual we were routing direct to St. Catherine's Point on the Isle of Wight. Just as we passed the Casquets lighthouse, I felt a judder. Jean had not felt it, but a moment later there was another one. She felt that, and then the engine started shaking.

With memories of the previous failure and enormous cost, I was not going to continue over water and turned right for Alderney then shut down the engine and glided in. Once down safely we phoned back to Guernsey to see if anyone could help get us home, as there is no maintenance facility on Alderney, and we would have been stuck.

Paul Smiddy was another BPPA pilot, and he was yet to leave Guernsey in his group-owned Robin. He and his son kindly stopped off and loaded us, but not our luggage into the back of the DR400 and took us to Rochester where he was based. Another kind soul at Rochester, Peter Liddle, gave us a lift to home where we could think about how to get the aircraft repaired and back.

After discussion with my engineer (it was still maintained at Little Staughton), he thought it must have been a magneto failure causing the rough running. He was happy to bring a couple of magnetos and replace mine on the spot but could not spare much time and demanded we collect him in something quick and fly him out there and back.

My first choice had been Tony Franchi and his Cessna 177 based at Earls Colne, who was a reliable friend. He was not available but recommended a buddy of his who would do us a favour. I drove to Staughton and we were picked up by a Saratoga, and once on Alderney were disappointed to find it was not the magneto at all, but the number 5 cylinder that had broken. The rocker gear had detached. Back to Staughton and home to order a new cylinder, and the Saratoga went back to Earls Colne. I had asked our pilot to let me know what my contribution should be, and he told me he would work it out.

I was quite disappointed to see an invoice arrive for over £500. It transpired that it was a group aircraft and he had invoiced the standard rate that he would pay when he flew it, with no contribution by himself. What made it worse, the hours charged for included some approaches he made at Southend on the way home. I paid with gritted teeth and looked for someone else to do the return visit.

My engineer, who was another Martin, was rather disappointed to be picked up in a Socata Rallye, but we got back to Alderney and replaced the cylinder. The Air Racing mob were there at the same time, briefing before their race and complained bitterly when we ran the engine up to ensure it was good. They just had to put up with the noise, because the airfield would be closed while they raced, and we had to get away – which the Rallye and Cessna did once we knew it was safe.

I was beginning to lose faith in my replacement engine. The O-300D is normally a smooth six-cylinder, but this was not the first pot to break. I had previously had to land at Panshanger when another one went, and we were talking £1000 a cylinder.

Shell "Fly Further"

I think it was in Pilot Magazine I saw the promotion for the Shell Fly Further scheme. The fuel and oil company wanted you to fly into airfields where their products were on sale. The rewards increased the more you visited. There was a total of twelve nominated fields, and at each field you had to get a landing fee receipt to say you had been there.

Once you had reached six you would receive a Shell baseball cap. At about nine there was a fine flight-bag on offer, and if you made all twelve you would be entered in a draw for the main prize. The airfields were scattered around the UK and included Jersey and Guernsey.

It ran over a few months and in my case took little effort. I was already visiting most of the required fields, so the baseball cap arrived in due course, then the flight-bag. Just before the scheme was due to close, I thought about how many people would have managed all twelve and decided it was probably none.

But I had ten, and the remaining ones were Peterborough Sibson and Fife. Why not, I thought. Sibson was just an hour away, but with a nasty headwind Fife was another three hours. Once the final receipt was in my hands, the same wind became a healthy 30-knot tailwind, and I was blown home non-stop in under three hours.

Three weeks later my theory was proved correct, and I was the happy recipient of a Garmin Pilot III GPS, which at the time was state of the art (and about £400). I kept my Garmin 90 attached to the yoke and positioned the Pilot III on the coaming. I had dual GPS!

South Africa

I had taken to South Africa on my first visit. My distributor welcomed me into his family, and soon Jean came too, and we stayed in a game park hotel with Richard and his wife. We fell in love with the place, the wildlife, and the people, and after another stay with them in a timeshare they had (in a different game park), I determined that I wanted more, and bought a timeshare in the same place – a week forever in February for just £600 plus annual maintenance levy. It was not long before I bought a second week in November.

I could combine business trips with my timeshare dates and could easily visit three times a year. Whilst I had not done any World Rally competitions since Sywell (I had focused on Precision) the 2003 Rally Championships were to be based at Pilanesberg with accommodation at Sun City – how could I refuse?

The problem with this type of rally is finding a navigator. I got lucky and Dick Nesbitt-Dufort was prepared to partner me. Dick came from an RAF family. During the war his father flew people in and out of France at night in a Lysander. (Read "The Black Lysander" if you can find a copy). Dick did not learn to fly until, as he himself confesses, he crashed his car when drunk. With a broken back and committed to a life of callipers and crutches, he decided to get over it and prove he could do something well.

He gained his licence and flew an Ercoupe, then Cherokees and finally he owned a Piper Colt which he kept at Heathfield. Part of the CAA test was that he had to prove he could fall out of the cockpit quickly if it were necessary to evacuate. It was much harder to heave him up into the back seat of the 172, where he would navigate from.

The BPPA organised practice rallies and we tested ourselves at Sibson and Haverfordwest before we set off for Johannesburg in another BA 747.

South Africa is good for many reasons, not least because of the exchange rate, but also because they drive on the correct side of the road, and Pilanesberg was only a couple of hours after landing. We had requested a 172 to hire and it was at a very reasonable rate. Provided we could show an FAI sporting licence (we did), the insurance would cover us for the competition, and we duly got the keys to ZS-JDO.

Practice days ensued. We needed these because the maps had been produced specially and were not like anything we had seen before. Almost monochrome, nearly everything was brown. Settlements were little dots. Rivers that were shown had dried out and the only way you could recognise them was the few trees and bushes that curved around where they had been. Roads were dirt tracks. The biggest features to recognise were mines with a pithead, and occasionally a hill that was being sliced up for marble. Easy, it was not.

We flew Pilanesberg to Pilanesberg, then to Rustenberg and return. Then the competition proper started from Rustenberg. The aircraft remained there, and we had to drive over each day. We did four judged competition days, each route being just over two hours. On the third day there was a spot landing touch and go at Allied Rivers – this was a strip constructed purely for the competition, marked out with the box. It was not shown on the map, but the route took you over it and when you found it, you used it. There was an allowance of ten minutes on that leg, so you had an idea where it was.

In a Rally you must fly at a constant groundspeed, rather than a constant airspeed as in Precision, so there are airspeed adjustments to be made to make sure you meet the minute marks which are all the same distance apart on each leg. Africa is a massive open space, and the distant mountains are high and deceptive (there are no heights on the competition map), so you must judge carefully and start climbing long before you reach them.

Each evening we handed back the GPS loggers and debriefed with the judges, then gathered as a team for our own debrief before an early night. It was hard work so no thoughts of partying, but we did allow ourselves a beer or two.

Once the four days had been flown, there was a reserve day that had not been necessary to use, and whilst Dick and I had to hand back the Cessna we had used, we managed to borrow another, ZS-MBP, so we could fly on our "day off". A strip that was marked on the map – a simple black line – was Mabula. This was an hour away, and where I had my timeshare. The British Team flew in very loose formation to land in the game park (after a beat-up to shift the wildebeest from the runway).

I had organised for us to go on a game drive and the rangers collected us from the strip. In three hours, we saw nearly all "the big five" – lion, elephant, rhino, and buffalo – only the leopard escaped us (but I had only ever seen one in the wild, when Jean had noticed one as it was sleeping in the shade of a tree, as we quietly freewheeled downhill, on a previous visit to the park). We then ate a leisurely lunch at the game lodge before the flight back to Rustenberg. Magical.

Back to the hotel at Pilanesberg, and it was time for the celebration dinner and closing ceremony, and as no surprise to anyone, the South Africa Team won everything. We did not care – we had had the most wonderful eighteen hours of flying and experienced the beauty of Africa.

Kilkenny Again

I am nothing if not persistent. Gradually my scores in the Navex improved, but so did others'. I was winning lots of other elements such as arrival, landings etc., but the grand prize eluded me – until Kinair 2000. Kilkenny has a lot of aviation history. In 1856 Lord Carlingford applied for patents for his "aerial chariot" which whilst patented, failed to fly. Others persevered, and in 1912 Denys Corbett-Wilson, a Kilkenny resident, achieved the first successful crossing of the Irish Sea in his Bleriot.

The organisers of Kinair present the overall winner with the Corbett-Wilson Trophy, which is a superb replica of a Bleriot in solid silver about 55cm long, standing on a wooden plinth. It is so valuable that after the photographs are taken, they take it back! But then the lucky winner is given his own little Bleriot in hallmarked sterling silver, but only 20cm long, and to be kept forever. In 2000 they had been too late to manufacture one of these, and I settled for a silver plate mounted on marble, with a Bleriot etched into it.

I so wanted one of those little Bleriots – the proper version. I finally got one in 2004 which was the last Kinair to be held. Pat Nolan, the airport manager, then retired and the new management did not carry it on. But a few years later, Pat and his buddy flew their Socata Rallye aircraft into Rochester to visit us and we chauffeured them around and wined and dined with them.

Fast forward even more years, and in 2015, Kilkenny were to put on a 50th anniversary air show. My resistance has always been low, and I contacted the new management to ask if we could attend and not only was it OK, but Pat and his family would be there.

It would be a long day with an early start. Too long and too early for Jean, but my buddy Rob Taylor (a Rochester

Arrow pilot) was happy to accompany me in Delta India. After just over three hours direct we arrived in time for the show and to see Pat who was as welcoming as ever. There were some fine displays which included an RV aerobatic team and the Irish Air Corps that used to have Cessna T-41s (a military 172) but now had Pilatus PC-9Ms – very swish.

We definitely needed Avgas and whilst the crew filled us to the top of our tanks, they couldn't take payment because of so much going on and the FBO being in use for display pilots. I scribbled my credit card details out and asked that they charge me next day or whenever they could, and eventually left to route home direct, arriving just an hour before dark.

To this day I have never been charged despite calling them several times to remind them. I was always told that the airfield manager would ring me back, but he never did. Did Pat pay, or did they just give me the fuel as they had done for the display pilots? One day I must visit there again and ask.

More than One Todd

Any pilot who has wanted to change his aircraft from burning Avgas to Mogas, will have no doubt heard of Todd Petersen. He has worked on creating STCs for just about every certified aircraft/engine combination possible to run on "Auto Fuel" and is happy to take your dollars and issue you with the appropriate paperwork, so you can save money.

After due investigation I never actually went this route. I deemed the inconvenience of having to find the right quality of petrol (perhaps having to test it?), transport it to the airfield, somehow pour it into a high-wing aircraft etc. to outweigh the potential savings. To say nothing of potential vapour locks and temperature restrictions.

But I did discover another Todd that I wanted to meet. This was Todd Peterson (son not sen), and he was in Wichita. I had read about a remarkable aircraft called the Cessna Skyshark that was developed to be the ultimate STOL in USA. It was basically a 182 with full width slotted flaps and movable spoilers along the wing that assisted roll control, and a high-lift canard with elevators positioned on the nose either side of the cowlings and behind the propellors slipstream.

With a 260HP engine fitted, it had amazingly short take-off and landing and if you find the old video that is available, it is quite remarkable. The aircraft was simply too expensive to produce, and Todd Peterson took most of the elements (not the moveable spoilers) and produced the Wren 460. One version even had a reversible thrust propellor for steeper approaches and shorter landings. Several Wrens were used by "Air America" for black ops, as even with maximum all-up weight, landing and take-off were only 300 feet.

The Wren Aircraft Company gained Cat II certification – because of the low approach speed it was allowed to land with quarter-mile visibility and 100-foot ceilings. They were trying to get clearance for landings in zero visibility when the company went bust in the late 1960s.

Like a phoenix, Todd emerged from the company's wreckage with the type certificate and after building a few Wrens, brought out the Peterson SE260. It was very similar, but now no longer with full width flaps. Despite that it would cruise at more than 150 knots and stall speed was just 35 knots. He still produces them today, and also the bush version – the Katmai - which sits on enormous tyres.

On another of my export trips I reached Wichita and met Todd. He was happy to demonstrate, and we flew amazing circuits inside the peri-track of the airfield. It would lift off at minimum speed and could immediately bank hard – all due to the canard. As an observation aircraft it could loiter for up to eleven hours at 50 knots. Imagine how well you could do in a precision competition (where you nominate the airspeed you will fly at)!

I wanted one. Whilst he would build a "new one" for you, based ideally on a 182Q, it would be a major, major expense and out of my range. You could buy the elements and convert one yourself, but it would never be allowed in UK. Only way would be to buy one second-hand in USA, ship/fly it over, and operate on the US register. But very few are ever resold because they are so good. It was all too complicated for me, and for now, I gave up.

I have since discovered there is just one in the UK. It is the lower powered 230HP but with the canard installed, still has remarkable performance. I have told the gentleman who keeps it on Barnards Farm that if he ever wants to sell her………

Troyes

Only three years after Pilanesberg, the 15th World Rally Flying Championship was to be closer to home, in Troyes, France. This meant economy and familiarity as we could fly our own aircraft rather than rent.

Despite South Africa, Dick was prepared to fly with me again, but preferred to make his own way there. From my Maypole base it was only two and a half hours, and he was there when I arrived. Next day we started the practice route, but after 80 minutes I needed to make a precautionary landing at Sezanne. The oil temperature needle was well into the red. Granted it was a hot day, and I had had the odd drip of oil hitting the front spat before, but now there was a lot. I always carried spare oil and we waited for it to cool, then topped up and finished the route – with a constant eye being kept on the gauge.

Back at Troyes we explained our dilemma, but the championship was starting the next day, and there was no engineer available. Our start times were all early morning which helped by the day being cooler, but each afternoon we would be wiping oil off the spat and pouring more into the engine. It made for nervous flying, but we got through.

Very happy that it was all over (we came 47th out of 65), Dick wished me goodbye and good luck over the Channel. Sure enough, I was topping up oil again at Lydd before reaching Maypole. The cooler weather of England helped and as long as I was prepared to keep pouring oil in, I could keep flying, which I did for almost two months.

But before I flew her again after returning home, being now totally dis-enamoured with the Continental, I started to investigate the options. The O-300D was 145HP and although generally smooth, struggled to climb (even after I had fitted a brand-new McCauley propellor to replace the original, which was deemed out of limits).

Air Plains Inc. near Wichita offered a conversion kit, whereby you could change everything firewall forward and end up with a factory-new Lycoming O-360A4M and Sensenich propellor. It was a lot of money, but the exchange rate at the time was just over $2 to the pound and the engine was reputed to be "bulletproof". And it only had four cylinders to break. More research was needed.

Whilst I was pondering, my good friend Alan Walton helped me out yet again with flying. He had moved on from the delightful Robin and bought a fabulous Cessna 195 which I had flown, but now he had a superb Rockwell Commander based at Conington. I drove up there, and after flights to Robin Hood, Fenland, and back to Conington I was signed off for the type. I had had my fix and could get to work on the CAA.

Persuading the CAA

The conversion was allowed in USA under a Supplementary Type Certificate. Anyone there was allowed to do it. But we were in EASA-land. I had to search for other aircraft that had a similar engine, as if it had been allowed before, they had to allow it again, didn't they?

I managed to find two. One was an imported 172 that had been converted before it came from USA and had been accepted onto the British register. Another had been rebuilt from a wreck and had been accepted. Armed with my information, my engineer approached the local CAA surveyor and he agreed.

Favours were called in. My shipping agent agreed a special rate to bring it over. We would use an end use certificate to avoid duty. Long discussions were had with Air Plains about the core they would expect in return. The shipping cost would be prohibitive, and it might not be to tolerances, so they agreed to reduce the core charge. Base kit, engine, export paperwork and core charge came to $38,125. The combined 257 Kg was brought over for less than £600, but the VAT payable was £3255.

We combined fitting the kit with the annual and at the same time the old heavy ADF which no longer worked, was removed to save weight, and a new weight and balance was done.

All told she was unavailable for three months, but it was winter so little chance of much happening anyway. But I did not waste the time. Using the CAA database, I contacted every UK owner of a Cessna with O-300D to offer the old engine, propellor and all the accessories. Whilst many wanted to cherry-pick bits and pieces, I was lucky enough to find someone who would take the lot for £5000. His O-300D would need zero-timing soon and he did not want the downtime. He would have mine rebuilt and sell his on when the time came. He also got an almost new propellor for his cash. The engine mount and other bits would be spares or he could sell on too.

The nett effect was that my factory-new engine and propellor (both with a 2000-hour TBO) had cost less than overhauling and zero-timing the Continental.

Much later she had new windows and screen fitted, and a new paint job. The performance meant she would be as fast as a Cessna 182, so I borrowed the latest 182 scheme from Cessna. If she was going to think she was a 182, she might as well look like one.

Test Flight

It was February 2007, and my good friend Alan Walton again came into play. An examiner now, he helped me find the necessary flight test procedures from the CAA. We downloaded the forms, planned the mission and went flying.

Basically, you measure performance against the flight manual, recording all the parameters and even plot the climb rate. The conclusion written and signed into the Check Flight Certificate states "Exceeds Stated Performance Manual". And boy, did she exceed it.

At 6000 feet with full power, she trued out at 130 knots, and the rev counter never went near the red. Climb rate was more than double the previous figure. I had a hot-rod 172.

To break in the new engine, I had to do 50 hours of hard flying, lots of full power and varying settings, and change the straight 80 oil at 25 hours. At 50 hours she went onto 15/50 oil and burning 36 litres an hour economy cruise was 110 knots (versus the old engine's 95 knots).

The other remarkable thing was how short a take-off run was needed. With 40 degrees of flap available you could land anywhere anyway, but now she could get out easily too. Being lighter than the more modern 172s that were also 180HP, she outperformed them too.

Rodney Blois, Chairman of the BPPA was so impressed that he decided to do the same with his G-AWMP, not knowing it would prevent hm flying for quite some time.

CAA yet again

Rodney duly installed the kit and asked for the CAA to sign it off. They would not. Their argument was that his Cessna was a Reims-built 172 and therefore not the 172 referred to in the STC (but so was mine!). He pointed out that I was signed off and enjoying my flying, and they countered by saying they had made a mistake, and I should not be, but they could not stop me now.

Mike Papa was grounded for nearly a year. I eventually managed to help by getting Cessna to admit that both USA and Reims built were the same, but it was like pulling teeth. Rodney finally got aloft and with the Flint tip-tanks he had fitted to increase fuel capacity enormously, made some of the longest flights I have ever heard of. My bladder would never get me to Tunisia in one hop.

It obviously rankled them that I had got away with it and eventually I had a phone call. They were concerned that I did not have a noise certificate. I did not. Because when the aircraft was built in 1969, no such thing existed, and there was never any retrospective requirement. "Ah, but the combination of engine and propellor you now have requires one", was the ploy.

Eventually a compromise was reached. There were others with the same mod flying happily in Europe (I knew of one Swedish one at least). If I applied to EASA for a Minor Change Approval for a fee of 300 Euro, if granted, they (the CAA) would give me a noise certificate for free. Anything for a quiet life, I stumped up the cash.

The engine had been flying since February 2007. By July 2009 I had an EASA approval, and a month later, a noise certificate. I was home free.

Where to use all that Power?

I had always liked finding new airstrips but now many more were accessible. I had lots of reasons to fly including local competitions, BPPA and air rallies, but the rallies were winding down, and of the majors, only Jersey and Guernsey still existed.

Then in 2010, the final Jersey International was held. Aviation was going through a lull again and numbers attending had dropped – indeed, for a period even Guernsey became a fly-in rather than a full-blown rally. The lower costs encouraged more to attend and eventually the Guernsey Rally re-emerged. Phew!

But Jersey was a real loss. We had attended 23 of them, were overall winners four times, and it was a rare year when we did not receive some silverware for a year's loan, and I had even won a flight in a Jet Provost. It would mean that we would not meet all the friends we had made that descended on the island annually as we did. New management had taken over and were not interested (sounds familiar?) and in years to come the club was to go bust. Happily, it has now re-emerged and hopefully will flourish.

The following year something new was on the horizon. An organisation announced the launch of RB12 – a Round Britain Rally to happen in 2012. Aircraft, powerboats, and supercars would all circumnavigate the UK, the pilots, skippers, and drivers meeting socially each evening at the nominated hotels. No doubt there would be lots of rich car and yacht owners willing to splash the cash, but to encourage aviators there was trial competition to take place at Bitburg, which we duly won – but the rally itself failed to attract enough people and was cancelled.

Guernsey continued, but the only other navigation exercises I could find (non-BPPA) was TOPNAV. This was the rebranded version of GNAV that I had done many years before. It was a different type of competition (the former had been a series of diversions using Wansborough-White's plastic navigation tools, now defunct). Now it was really a regular navigation competition, but it was necessary to keep a log of timings and events and how and why course corrections were made, notes about airspace etc – all to be submitted and judged later.

I recruited my Arrow-flying buddy, Rob Taylor to assist with the log, and flew the course from White Waltham. We could not make the first day, so were allowed to try the next, and couldn't have chosen a worse day. The course took almost two hours avoiding control zones and at one stage we were IMC for quite some time in an absolute deluge. But we recovered and regained the route, Rob wrote everything down, and eventually we were invited to a presentation at the Royal Institute of Navigation, where Prince Philip presented us with the winning trophies.

Five years later, Rob and I tried again from my place of learning to fly, Conington, and although we won the Conington heat, we did not get the overall win (heats were held from four or five different airfields). But it was still nice to meet Princess Anne for our certificates.

Big and Very Small Airfields

Rob's Arrow was a mini airliner. He had all manner of expensive kit (even music) and he liked big airports. Would I like to sit in, and we could fly into Stansted? It must have been a rhetorical question because I jumped at the chance. Rob organised permissions and negotiated with Harrods Aviation, who would handle us, and we were set.

Except the Arrow went unserviceable. With booking made, the alternative was to go in my Cessna. Thus, it was me making the Ryanair wait whilst we landed and then taxying past an executive 747 owned by a Saudi Prince to the Harrods hangar. It was the first London airport I had landed at for many years (because prices by now were prohibitive) and I enjoyed getting the Harrods stamp in my logbook.

Being rather younger than me, Rob is my go-to man for technical stuff. Upcoming was to be the Throckmorton Air Show put on at the old site of RAF Pershore. Because the concrete of Pershore is so broken up and pot-holed it could not be used, the organisers were going to cut two grass strips for visitors to attend. They were to be 275m and 370m long – but there was a forest at the threshold of the 370m, so effectively they were both the shorter length.

We determined we better do some short field practice to ensure we were comfortable, and that is when Rob's technical bent came to the fore. Using GPS, he found he could measure exactly both the take-off run and ground roll to a full stop of my Cessna. We practiced at Rochester and the final result was a full stop in 77m and take-off in 133m. We booked our slot at Throckmorton.

On the day there was a stonking gusty crosswind on both runways, but it slightly favoured over the trees to land, which we duly did. There were not many people that did manage to land. This included the Aerosuperbatics Team (aka Crunchie/Utterly Butterly etc.) in their 450HP Stearmans. They gave a great display but after a couple of landing attempts thought better of it and returned to Rendcomb. A great day was had, and it was another one that I know I could not have done with the old engine.

Islands

One of the greatest things about aeroplanes is that they can pass over water and take you to nearby islands. Whilst the Channel Islands were amongst my favourites, there were Scottish and Irish varieties to try, and I had done a lot of that, but I had never been to Lundy.

Pete White organises a fly-in there once a year, and it is he that you must speak to for permission. If you have not visited previously, you are grilled about what aircraft and your experience as it is not the easiest of strips, and you fly in at your own risk. It is about 400m of rough grass (and often stones which Pete tries to clear the day before the fly-in) and it is uphill with a fair amount of sheep droppings. Most of the visitors are traditional taildraggers, PFA types, or microlights that need little runway.

Once I explained I had a 172 I was informed of a previous 172 that being heavy, had failed to take off and burned. I countered with how I would be light, only 2 persons on board, and I had a bigger more powerful engine which had got me into and out of many strips. Accepted, I made my first visit of many.

Leaving Rochester with full tanks, by the time we reached the island I had burnt well over half my fuel, and there were no problems. The island can be walked in a short time, which we did, but we were too late in the year to see the puffins. I would need to try again.

On the same day, the local strut had organised a fly-in at Treborough (near Minehead) which I could not find on any map and when we had flown overhead the co-ordinates we were given, on the way to Lundy, we could not see an airfield.

Leaving Lundy, we had to go to Eaglescott to refuel and then tried to find Treborough. This time it was obvious because it was a farm field now filled with PFA aircraft. Not an airfield, a farm field. We landed in a cloud of dust, and I think I was the only aircraft with a nosewheel.

Wanting to return home by a different route, we stopped off at Old Sarum to wipe the dust from the aircraft.

Runways are Always Important

In a similar theme, it is always good that if you land somewhere, that you can take off from there too. Sometimes this can be a problem, particularly if the airfield only has one runway and someone does something inconvenient.

First experience of this had been at Retford/Gamston. We were simply visiting and were about to fuel when a very smart Twin Comanche (G-BLOR) gave a demonstration flight to a prospective buyer. Satisfied that the punter knew his stuff the owner then told him to go off and fly for half an hour and "come back and make an offer".

Oscar Romeo reappeared after we had refuelled, and we watched his excellent controlled approach. It would have been a perfect flight except that both propellors chopped into the tarmac - there was no undercarriage down, and it slid along on its belly. The pictures I have depict the owner diving into the cockpit to see if the gear handle had been used, whilst the shocked (and embarrassed) pilot (no longer a prospective purchaser) holds his face in his hands in disbelief.

With two shock-loaded engines and destroyed propellors she was written off by the insurance company, but now with new engines and propellors and re-skinned she flies happily in the West Country. We had had to wait around whilst she was pulled off the runway by the fire truck, but at least we were allowed to leave before the AAIB arrived.

We spent many happy years flying into and out of Earls Colne, and boy, has it changed now? It now has a smart tarmac runway as well as the parallel grass, and there is excellent hard-standing, clubhouse and hangars next to the threshold of runway 06. That did not use to be the case. The clubhouse used to be due south of the threshold of runway 24, at the bottom of the airfield peritrack. You taxied up the peritrack to reach the runway, and the tarmac was just wide enough for a 172's undercarriage, and just far enough away that your wing did not snag the trees, which were supposed to protect you from flying golf balls from the club next door (which they did most of the time).

In boggy conditions (and with great care) the peritrack became a runway. It was not safe to use for landing being so narrow and close to trees, but you could get out, and take your chances landing back on the then grass-only runway. It has all changed now, with the golf club expanded, and a hotel built near where the old clubhouse used to be, and with one of the newest tarmac runways in the country, it is a great place to fly.

But it is not just mud that prevents getting airborne (although I do remember once having to take off from Rochester from the southern parking area – which was slightly elevated and a touch drier - and had to be airborne before I reached the runway).

Having enjoyed a visit to Bruntingthorpe for their Cold War Jets Day, we needed to get away but were stymied by a parade of Lightnings going up and down the runway that would last a considerable time. We were allowed to take off from a fine taxiway, nicely shaded from a strong crosswind by some very high trees. A successful departure, but quite a curl of wind as we crested above the trees. There is a lot to be said for unlicensed aerodromes and the freedom they enjoy.

A much more recent incident was at Stoke Golding. A fly-in had been planned but due to the pandemic, organised events had to be cancelled and the organisers duly complied and informed all those that had booked a place. However, the airfield was still open to visitors quite legally, and spookily over seventy aircraft happened to turn up on the day that had been planned for the fly-in. No doubt we had all done our planning and thought we might as well use it?

I had arrived early and was parked about 100m from the end of the landing runway. I was stood by the runway when a Pelican PL touched down by me with no signs of slowing. Instead of putting the power on again he rushed through the hedge at the end and fell into a deep ditch full of trees. Fortunately, pilot and passenger had no serious injuries, but they were trapped for some time as the trees prevented access to the doors.

The airfield was immediately closed to await the AAIB. The airfield owner had been doing aerobatics and could not land back. He gave a spirited performance overhead while we twiddled our thumbs, and eventually had to go and land elsewhere. Some hours later we were told we could depart on the reciprocal runway, and the scene was similar to a Battle of Britain scramble as people ran to their machines.

The Pelican aircraft (written off after this, its second accident) was G-MPAC – somehow a fitting registration?

The Vulcan

In my schooldays I used to cycle to Avro at Woodford where they were being produced. I wrote earlier about watching them scramble at Finningley, and at whatever air show they appeared at, they were always a favourite of mine.

When Eddie and I had participated in the World Air Rally Championships at Sywell, on one leg Eddie had told me to keep the turn on, and we were closely overtaken by a Vulcan at the same height (even though they had retired from active service by then). At Wellesbourne we had a Vulcan on permanent static exhibit, but with systems being maintained by volunteers and it would make high-speed runs from time to time, which were impressive.

Other Vulcans were scattered around the country but un-moving, until the Vulcan to the Sky campaign managed to restore and fly XH558 in 2007. There followed eight glorious years of seeing her fly at events around the country, whenever I could. But 11 October 2018 she made her last, a farewell flight around Great Britain. Most people flocked to the nearest airfield she would appear at, and my nearest was North Weald where I landed to watch her fly past. But she was on a route around the country, and after she departed, I had just enough time to fly across to Gloucester where she would appear about an hour later.

On parking, I was greeted by a fellow rallyist Adrian Chipp (from Croft Farm). "I thought you'd be bloody here" he said. I stood with Adrian and journalist/author Geoff Jones (with whom I had written about rallying, and who had managed to get me a flight in a Dragon Rapide at Guernsey) and we watched the final display. I am certain it was not only me with a tear in the eye.

It was the first time I had seen Geoff since I flew him to Belle Vue airfield in Devon for the celebration of Howard

Cox, three years earlier. Howard was previously a BPPA pilot, but he had perished after an engine fire in his Bede BD5 on the way to the Foynes Air Show in Eire. There was no funeral, but we gathered in the village hall, and his buddies from the Devon strut made a "missing man" flyby over the hall. Very tasteful, and we all recounted stories of what a generous type he was.

I left Gloucester once the Vulcan had gone, and I never saw Geoff again – he passed away not long after. Aviation allows you to meet some wonderful people, but some go missing.

I hate Cessna 150s

I had learnt on 152s which were quite mannerly, but 150s are something else. I had had a bad experience with one in Thailand but now I was going to have to fly one for a week.

In September 2016 the World Air Rally Championships were held at Santa Cruz, Portugal. Rodney Blois, our Chairman, with his new long-range Cessna decided to fly there himself, but us mere mortals did not have the time (or long-range bladders) so went scheduled and hired. Our airliners stayed out of restricted airspace en route, which is more than can be said for Rodney and Judith, who found themselves with F-16s either side of them. After explaining what he was doing in Portugal, the same F-16s came and gave the assembled nations' teams a display. Nice one, Roddy!

We had asked for a 172, but there was not one on offer. Instead, we were allocated the awful CS-APA, a 150, and were to share its use with one of the Portuguese teams. My navigator this time was Malcom Evans – the other Cessna pilot who had competed for the Piper Cup in Bournemouth.

The organisers kept telling us how Papa Alpha was the best aircraft the club owned, but after their team and ourselves had done our practice days, our Portuguese competitors somehow found a French-registered 152 they would fly instead. Our sharing partners were now a Danish team.

Papa Alpha looked attractive enough with a newish paint scheme, but as soon as you started moving, the windows would spring open of their own volition. If you are trying to manage maps and have photographs BluTack'd all over the dashboard, this is not helpful and we resorted to gaffer tape to try to keep them shut, with only limited success.

Once actually in the air, any load applied by moving the yoke backwards and the doors would pop open. Taping yourself into an aeroplane is not a good idea, so we settled on just one door (we would need one to open to be passed the route to plot, twenty minutes before we took off, as the window was taped shut).

We did the competition like that, but the distraction of windows and doors opening at will despite our efforts was somewhat off-putting. On the penultimate competition day, I was very early for a turning point. Seconds are more important than targets spotted, so I slowed and slowed. Had I been in my 172 with the droopy wingtips I could have hung in the air as the stall speed is so slow, but now I was in Papa Alpha.

The spin took me completely by surprise – I had not done a spin since I was in the Air Cadets. If it were not for Malcolm shouting at me to unload and then kicking the rudder in the right direction, there could have been a very different outcome. As it was, we pulled out, regained track, and completed the course, resolving not to tell anybody about my mistake.

We did not get away with it of course, because in the debrief when we downloaded the logger, the judges spotted it, and we were given maximum penalties for orbiting. I still have the readout from the logger, and it shows the point the stall happened at 35 knots groundspeed (we had a headwind and design stall speed is 42 knots). With full flap my 172 would still be flying until after it was off the clock at 38 mph. We took 27 seconds to fully recover and in that brief time, we had dropped from 1465 feet to 1026 feet, and there was a hill below us.

Next day was the last competition day and we had Papa Alpha in the morning, and the Danes were to take her in the afternoon. Although we did our best, if I was early at any turning point, we stayed early. Once bitten......

That afternoon, the Danes finished their competition early by dead-sticking her into a ploughed field when the engine failed. Fortunately, they walked away. I hate Cessna 150s.

Another Change in Direction

A year before Portugal I had reached retirement age. My colleagues were surprised, even shocked, that I actually left the company because I had a good job travelling the world, they thought. But time away and time on airliners prevents you flying yourself. It was true I had enjoyed being pampered on board. I had discovered you could go completely round the world in business class for just £3000, and I was not paying.

A typical trip would be going to our office in Dubai, then on to Singapore for a few days with side trips to Malaysia and Thailand. Then a big push to Australia, followed by New Zealand, and then keep going to LA, and New York, before coming home. I filled passports rapidly and could never spend all the airmiles accrued because I was on aeroplanes most of the time.

I wanted more time for Jean and myself. I am still not certain if Jean wanted quite so much time together, but as an indicator, there is never any objection to my going off flying for the day.

What to do with all this free time? All the usual things of course, but by now most air rallies were no more. Guernsey was about the last and pre-COVID, I made my 31st entry. Hopefully, the planned rally in 2021 will happen. The LAA rallies continue but these are really the biggest fly-in you can attend (apart from Oshkosh), and although I always go and browse the stalls and aircraft, I am neither an LAA member nor a builder.

What I miss from the "gin and tonic" rallies is the amazing people we had met and had fun with. So many characters – like Jim King, who landed his Piper Colt G-ASSE in a cow pasture to pick up Margaret en route and was given a special award for "the pilot who pulled himself out of the most s*** to get here". Or Farmer Adrian Chipp who was always worrying about his cows and would bring his mate, Bruce, if he had not got a current "squeeze" (but I expect to see him if Guernsey does happen again). Des Russell, as already mentioned. So many others from all over UK and overseas...

But I needed some other purpose to fly and discovered Air Search.

Ron Armitage

Amongst the down-trodden residents at Maypole was Ron and his better half, Sandra. Whilst I was a resident too, I seemed to remain a "new boy" to many of the others, as they were older (more traditional aviators with heritage aircraft) and I was just a Cessna-driver. But Ron and Sandra were more welcoming.

After retirement I could go flying any day of the week, and weekdays made sense as there was less flying school action at Rochester and little holding necessary. But a couple of times a month the café would be filled with a motley crew, mainly seniors, in uniform. Ron and Sandra were amongst them.

And so it was, I joined Air Search. A voluntary organisation, Air Search is made up of a mix of pilots and observers who enjoy meeting twice a month to train and are available to help whoever needs them. Air Search was a spin-off from a similar organisation, and others exist under names like Civil Air Patrol and Sky Watch. The Civil Air Patrol in the USA is a paid organisation, whereas Air Search is completely self-funded by the members. The pilots donate their time and costs of flying their aircraft, and the observers make a small contribution whenever they fly. The training sessions are usually Tuesdays and members need to be available for "missions" when required. No wonder there were so many seniors.

For the organisation to have a real function it needs agreement with the local authorities and in Kent we are blessed with an active and well-organised Resilience Forum run by the County Council. Kent Voluntary Services Emergency Group brings together all the emergency services and volunteer organisations that can offer real assistance.

For Air Search that means we can be asked to do all manner of tasks, whether photographing traffic, fires, floods, or exercises being carried out by the other services. The Air Search motto is "search, locate, report" and to teach us how to do it, was Ron Armitage our training officer.

Ron flies a Huskie and Sandra uses her camera skills from the rear seat. I am not completely sure if Ron is a real sadist, but he would create some devilish operations for us to try and then berate us when we got them wrong. If the weather were inclement, these would be desk-top and mainly landmark identification on varying maps to help us get our head round differing scales.

Safety and planning were also high on the syllabus, and then came the flying. Sector searches were hard to do, but a creeping line search could be programmed into the Garmin 496, and to cover a hundred square nautical miles might take an hour once on task.

We would be tasked to find a particular building or ground feature and on occasions, downed aircraft. It is surprising how many Kent residents have a piece of militaria in their back gardens. With Ron flying low and slow, Sandra would have taken the targets and the observers had their work cut out.

I had a new purpose to fly! Missions included pollution exercises, filming evacuation of Romney Marsh (Operation Surge), a simulated train crash, photographing Dungeness nuclear power station and surroundings, and even Operation Vulcan where after Grenfell, we photographed blocks of flats throughout the county and the escape routes around them.

Prior to my joining, Ron had done a photographic survey of the myriad number of airstrips in Kent, and these were used by Border Force – and we looked for more. We also assisted with filming public information films about awareness of suspicious aviation activity. Delta India was a star (but not really guilty of bringing in an illegal immigrant – it was Alex, one of our own, in the hoodie).

Kent Police and the (very nice) CAA

Catherine is the volunteer liaison officer for KP, and active within KVSEG (the resilience forum). Familiar with our activities and with an eye on Brexit and other situations, felt we could do more for the police.

The stopper would be communication. They wanted to be able to talk to us directly, but we could not use anything other than our licensed radios, and the Airwave radios used by police helicopters would mean massive expense for installation and certification. I had to talk to my friends(?) at the CAA.

Surprisingly, they were more than helpful. After ensuring nothing we were doing was for commercial purposes, they reaffirmed Air Search was legal to operate on private licences. Then following a meeting down at Gatwick, they allocated an Ops frequency we could use. Being Ops rather than an air traffic service, it could be operated by unlicensed personnel on the ground, and they gave approval for a base station at Police HQ, which was duly installed.

Now prepared, we started the process of becoming Community Policing Volunteers. Quite a long process with vetting involved, it eventually came together and a dozen of us (a mix of pilots and observers) were ready to go.

This was going to be fun and confidential (and I will not mention the frequency - for obvious reasons). Hopefully, a bonus is going to be that I can now enter competitions put on by the British Police Flying Association – the Polair Competitions - because I now have a force number!

Gaining from GAINS

It is very rare that the CAA will allow someone to pay a private pilot to fly, but this happened in 2019. An email received from AOPA suggested they were looking for pilots to fly unusual approaches, in order to prove GPS possibilities. The project was funded by the SESAR 2020 programme, and it was called GAINS – General Aviation Improvement in Navigations and Surveillance. Those acronyms again!

A survey needed to be completed which questioned your experience, aircraft and equipment and should you be accepted, you would be reimbursed for not only flying approaches at various southern airfields, but also for reaching those fields – and it would cover all costs including fuel, maintenance, insurance – you simply said what your overall flying costs were (and any landing fees would be covered too). The flights would be flown in VFR conditions, but on instruments and a safety pilot was required.

I applied of course, nominating Rob as my safety pilot, and he applied nominating me as his. I never heard any more directly as my limited panel was presumably not deemed high-tech enough, whereas Rob's was all-singing and all-dancing. He had spent a small fortune on GTN650, Garmin 430, ADSB transponder etcetera and was just what they wanted. It took an overlong time to organise as approvals needed to be gained to insert a different chip into the GTN650 which would allow the approaches.

We were to fly approaches at Sywell, Duxford and Cambridge (with loggers to record how well we did) - which we duly did, but before we could get to that stage, Rob hit a snag. He still did not have his IR/R rating, whereas I did. The organisers agreed that we could share flying his aircraft, with myself doing the approaches and Rob would be reimbursed for all the costs we incurred.

The approaches varied considerably in style and difficulty and many involved flying curves for terrain or airspace avoidance.

I believe there were up to twenty people involved flying approaches here and there, and many of the others were highly experienced IR-rated pilots. Our logger probably did not record tracks as good as theirs, but from each approach we could have landed safely despite my unfamiliarity with the kit. It was a real team effort by the two of us.

Rob had done more flying than me, just positioning the aircraft but I still logged a couple of hours instrument flying – all free. I believe the overall cost reimbursed to Rob was somewhere north of £2000. Not to be sniffed at, but it took an incredibly long time to be paid out.

The whole exercise had been very expensive for the organisers but gave good results. Where it goes from here is now in some doubt, as after Brexit we no longer have EGNOS, the European satellite system, available to us (officially at least). Watch this space.

Another Evans

Whilst all this was going on, I was still wanting to find new places to fly to.

In 2016 I had mentioned to Rob that I was reaching 300 airfields logged, and he had asked me to send him the spreadsheet so he could compare. That week, Rob accompanied me to number 300. On our return, I was called to the tower at Rochester by Kelvin, the airfield manager who looked as if he was going to tear a strip off me. With a look like thunder, he enquired where had we been and had we enjoyed ourselves (his tone suggested I had done something very wrong). I was terribly relieved when he then presented me with a certificate listing all 300 airfields, countries visited, how long I had owned the aircraft etc. Nice one, Rob and Kelvin.

When Marconi pulled out of Rochester and no longer had their twin based there, the lease had come up for grabs and it looked as if the airfield could be sold for housing. Neither pilots nor nearby residents wanted that and so PAFRA was formed (Pilots and Friends of Rochester Airport). After campaigning a new company was formed and a short-term lease obtained (later to be replaced with a longer one).

PAFRA remains to this day and is a social club organising fly-outs on both weekdays and weekends. On one such trip a non-pilot member was looking for a spare seat, and that is how I met Colin Evans.

Since then, we have done a remarkable amount of flying together. He is a generous sort when it comes to helping out with costs, and like me wants to find places new, interesting aircraft and appreciates the wonderful people who make us welcome at strips whenever we find a new one. Although not a pilot (he wanted to be, but medical reasons prevented him) he logs all his trips and now has more than 1000 hours – more than most PPLs.

Colin is also a member at the Brooklands Museum. The old runway there has been gone for many years, but just a few times a year they have a fly-in. There is 400m of not very good grass between the museum and Mercedes World and they invite vintage aircraft to visit, although they have never achieved very many due to a combination of weather and performance needs. Having read about this and it being the Cessna's 50th year (is that vintage enough?), I begged for an invite and got it.

On the day, Colin and I flew in and were the second aircraft to arrive (apart from the camera ship helicopter they used). Whilst we were overhead, Tim had flown his Puss Moth in from Hungerford and made a brave effort of landing in the gusty crosswind. His efforts make remarkable viewing on YouTube, where you can find the Brooklands Museum Aviation Day and Fly-in August 2019. We landed shortly after and then Tim was so worried about the gusty wind that he folded up the wings of the Puss Moth.

Checking in at the control desk to receive our packed lunch and another very special logbook stamp, the lady behind the desk said "Oh, you're the Cessna – that's the one aircraft I bet wouldn't be able to land". Ha! In fact, it seemed obvious no-one else would make it in, and eventually we departed around lunchtime.

We missed the Pitts that later arrived to be the only other aircraft to arrive. Ever since, I have wanted to return and have a waiting list of passengers that want to come, but up until now the pandemic has stopped any recurrence.

When lockdown struck, and I could not fly, to keep my brain active I wrote an aviation crime thriller (The Airborne Ghost – copies may still be available). Colin was one of the stars, and many of my acquaintances featured. The novella received pretty good acclaim from various magazines but was very much written for pilots and included a lot of technical detail, so will never reach a wider audience and make my fortune.

What Happens Next

I am uncertain how to finish this memoir - because it is not finished yet – or at least my flying is not. I will continue for as long as possible, working for the emergency services whenever needed, searching out new strips and fun events when not.

Currently, Rochester Airport is in the throes of reconstruction. The pandemic has prevented dual flying (except with household members) up until now. Hopefully by the time this is published that will have changed and we will have our freedom back.

Now with more than 400 airfields logged, I am aiming for 500. With more than 3000 hours flown I am uncertain if I will reach the next significant number but am determined to try. Jean has great understanding about my Cessna mistress – she knows I want to spend time (and most of my money) on her, but Delta India is getting older too….

When I bought my faithful Cessna, I was 35, she was 17 – half my age. By 2006, I was 55, she was 37 – two thirds of my age. Now, I am 70 and she is 52 – three-quarters of my age. It seems obvious that she is catching up with me, and I have determined that we will keep flying together until we are the same age - or until one of us can no longer pass our annual inspection. It has always been and remains fun despite the occasional setback.

P.S. I just heard there is now a 2-seat Hurricane. Now that is something I would like to fly….

Last Word

Thank you for reading Pilots Progress. I hope you have enjoyed it as much as I did, recalling my experiences. If you have any questions, or would like to contact me about any matter, please email me at airsearch2@outlook.com.

And if you have enjoyed it, please consider leaving a two-sentence review on Amazon. Amazon reviews are what makes the world go round for writers!

Also by Martin Leusby

The aviation thriller "The Airborne Ghost" is 20,000 words – a novella which is 85% true and tells the story of a British private pilot visiting Paris - where he sees something that results in an airborne pursuit across Europe and puts him in a life-threatening situation.

Written primarily for other pilots, who will understand the technicalities of both the detective work and the journey, it will be appreciated by anyone with an aviation interest who enjoys a real page-turner!

The question is.......will he get back safely?

GLOSSARY

AAIB Air Accident Investigation Board

ADF Automatic Direction Finder (points towards NDB beacons)

ADSB transponder radio equipment to identify you to ATC

Annual once yearly aircraft inspection and maintenance

AOPA Aircraft Owners & Pilots Association

ATC Air Traffic Control or Air Training Corps

ATCO Air Traffic Control Officer

ATPL Airline Transport Pilot Licence

ATZ Aerodrome Traffic Zone

BPPA British Precision Pilots Association

CAA Civil Aviation Authority

C of A Certificate of Airworthiness

CB Cumulonimbus – a thunder cloud

CFI Chief Flying Instructor

Charlie Fox Delta identifier CFD for NDB beacon at Cranfield

Check Six Look behind you (refers to six o'clock)

Chapter 11 company defence against creditors (similar to administration in UK)

Class 1 certificate necessary medical to become a commercial pilot

Delta India callsign of my aircraft G-AXDI

DME Distance Measuring Equipment

EASA European Union Aviation Safety Agency

EGSR Airfield Identifier for Earls Colne

FAI Fédération Aéronautique Internationale - aviation sporting body association

FIR Flight Information Region

FL75 Flight Level 7500 feet (measured against a standard pressure setting)

Foggles frosted glasses that only allow the pilot to see instruments (for training purposes)

GAPAN Guild of Air Pilots and Navigators became The Honourable Company of Air Pilots

Garmin manufacturer of GPS equipment

Glide Slope the indicated correct path to descend when using ILS

GPS Global Positioning System

HMRC Her Majesty's Revenue and Customs

HNC Higher National Certificate

HSI Horizontal Situation Indicator

IFR Instrument Flight Rules

ILS Instrument Landing System

IMC Instrument Meteorological Conditions – a rating to allow flight in non-VFR conditions

IR Instrument Rating – higher qualification than IMC

IR/R new name for the IMC

KISM Airport Identifier for Kissimmee Airport

Knots or Kts speed in nautical miles per hour

LAA Light Aircraft Association – new name for PFA

MAUW Maximum All Up Weight

MoD Bedford Ministry of Defence airfield – now privately operated

NM or Nautical Mile equivalent to 1.15 statute miles

PAR Precision Approach Radar – a talkdown procedure, includes height and direction

PFA Popular Flying Association – became the LAA

PPL Private Pilot Licence

RAF(VR) Voluntary Reserve members of the RAF

Reims-built Cessnas were built in France under licence from Cessna USA

RT Radiotelephony (or radio transmissions)

Special VFR permission to fly in conditions of reduced visibility

SRA Surveillance Radar Approach – a talkdown procedure without measuring height

SSFA Soldier Seaman and Airman's Family Association

STC Supplementary Type Certificate – allows alterations from original design

STOL Short Take-Off and Landing

Strasser Scheme a safety initiative that allows aircraft to land free if diverted due weather

TAP Transportes Aéreos Portgueses – now renamed Air Portugal

TBO Time Before Overhaul – hours before must be renewed/maintained

VNE Velocity Never Exceed – the maximum speed for an airframe without damage

VFR Visual Flight Rules

VHF Very High Frequency (radio transmissions)

VOLMET meteorological information for aircraft in flight by radio

VOR VHF Omnidirectional Range – a beacon showing radials (directions from beacon in magnetic degrees)

Vortrack an old-fashioned navigational device once used with VORs

Whizz-wheel a circular slide-rule used for aviation calculations such as tracks and speeds

Zero-timing refurbishment of an engine to bring back to as new tolerances